Learning from Summer

Effects of Voluntary Summer Learning on Low-Income Urban Youth

Catherine H. Augustine, Jennifer Sloan McCombs, John F. Pane,
Heather L. Schwartz, Jonathan Schweig, Andrew McEachin, Kyle Siler-Evans

Commissioned by

The Wallace Foundation

Supporting ideas.
Sharing solutions.
Expanding opportunities.

For more information on this publication, visit www.rand.org/t/RR1557

Library of Congress Cataloging-in-Publication Data is available for this publication.
ISBN: 978-0-8330-9660-9

Published by the RAND Corporation, Santa Monica, Calif.
© Copyright 2016 RAND Corporation
RAND® is a registered trademark.

Cover photos: Fotolia

Support RAND
Make a tax-deductible charitable contribution at
www.rand.org/giving/contribute

www.rand.org

Preface

Research has determined that low-income students lose ground to more affluent peers over the summer. Other research has shown that some summer learning programs can benefit students, but we know very little about whether voluntary, district-led summer programs can improve outcomes among low-income students.

To fill this gap and to expand summer program opportunities for students in urban districts, The Wallace Foundation launched the National Summer Learning Project in 2011. As part of the overarching project, this six-year study offers the first-ever assessment of the effectiveness of voluntary, district-led summer learning programs offered at no cost to low-income, urban, elementary students. The study, conducted by the RAND Corporation, uses a randomized controlled trial and other analytic methods to assess the effects of district-led programs on academic achievement, social-emotional competencies, and behavior over the near and long term. All students in the study were in the third grade as of spring 2013 and enrolled in a public school in one of five urban districts: Boston; Dallas; Duval County, Florida; Pittsburgh; or Rochester, New York.

The study follows these students from third to seventh grade. Our primary focus is on academic outcomes, but we also examine students' social-emotional outcomes, behavior, and attendance. We also collected extensive data about the summer programs to help us examine how implementation is related to program effects and to develop operational guidance for summer program leaders.

This report is the third in a series that will result from the study. It examines student outcomes at four different time points: in fall 2013, at the end of the 2013–2014 school year, in fall 2014 after the second summer of programming, and at the end of the 2014–2015 school year. The first report, *Getting to Work on Summer Learning: Recommended Practices for Success* (Augustine et al., 2013), offered lessons learned from detailed formative evaluations of the district programs in summer 2011. These evaluations, shared originally with districts in fall 2011, were designed to help summer program leaders improve the programs they offered in 2012. RAND completed another set of evaluations of the summer 2012 programs so that the districts could further strengthen their programs by summer 2013, when we launched a randomized controlled trial to assess effects on student performance. The second report, *Ready for Fall? Near-Term Effects of Voluntary Summer Learning Programs on Low-Income Stu-*

dents' Learning Opportunities and Outcomes (McCombs, Pane, et al., 2014), looked at how students in this study performed on mathematics, reading, and social-emotional assessments in fall 2013. In a fourth and final report, we will again examine student outcomes at the end of the 2016–2017 school year, when the students complete seventh grade.

This research has been conducted by RAND Education, a unit of the RAND Corporation that conducts research on prekindergarten, K–12, and higher education issues, such as preschool quality rating systems, assessment and accountability, teacher and leader effectiveness, school improvement, out-of-school time, educational technology, and higher education cost and completion.

This study is sponsored by The Wallace Foundation, which seeks to support and share effective ideas and practices to foster improvements in learning and enrichment for disadvantaged children and the vitality of the arts for everyone. Its current objectives are to improve the quality of schools, primarily by developing and placing effective principals in high-need schools; improve the quality of and access to after-school programs through coordinated city systems and by strengthening the financial management skills of providers; reimagine and expand learning time during the traditional school day and year, as well as during the summer months; expand access to arts learning; and develop audiences for the arts. For more information and research on these and other related topics, please visit The Foundation's Knowledge Center at www.wallacefoundation.org.

Contents

Figures and Tables

Figures

Tables

Summary

Summer learning programs have the potential to mitigate the academic achievement gap between students from low-income and higher-income households. Although recent research is inconclusive on whether students experience a loss of achievement over the summer, it is clear that low-income students learn less than their wealthier peers over an entire school year and that part of the disadvantage occurs over the summer. Low-income children also have fewer opportunities for cultural, athletic, and other stimulating summer activities than their more-affluent peers.

Evidence on summer program effectiveness comes mainly from studies of mandatory district-run programs and small, voluntary programs offered primarily by nonprofit organizations. Until this study, there has been little research on whether voluntary district-run summer learning programs can improve academic, behavioral, and social-emotional outcomes for low-income, urban youth, both in the near and long term.

The National Summer Learning Study

The Wallace Foundation launched the National Summer Learning Project in 2011 to fill this gap in the research base and to expand summer program opportunities for students in urban districts. As a part of this project, The Foundation sponsored the RAND Corporation to conduct a study of district-led, voluntary summer programs in five school districts—Boston; Dallas; Duval County, Florida; Pittsburgh; and Rochester, New York—and assess their effects on more than 3,000 students.

We examined these effects using several methods, including a randomized controlled trial on a cohort of students who were third-graders in spring 2013. This report presents findings on the effects of two consecutive summers of programming in 2013 and 2014 on language arts and mathematics learning and on less-studied outcomes—student behavior and social-emotional competence—in both the near term (the fall after each summer program) and the longer term (through spring 2015). Because the study is longitudinal and ongoing, the results presented in this interim report are not yet complete: We will be tracking student outcomes through spring 2017.

Although districts made their own choices about some aspects of their programs, such as curriculum, they agreed to incorporate a common set of elements:

- voluntary, full-day programming combining academics and enrichment for five days per week for no less than five weeks of the summer
- at least three hours of instruction (language arts and mathematics) per day
- small class sizes of no more than 15 students per adult
- no fee to families for participation
- free transportation and meals.

In spring 2013, we randomly assigned applicants to the summer program into two groups: one group (the treatment group) was admitted to two summers of programming (2013 and 2014) and the other (the control group) was not. Control group students and their families received lists of other free and low-cost summer program options in their community; in one district, families in the control group also were offered a stipend to help defray program costs.

Randomized controlled trials are the most rigorous method of causal analysis because the lottery-like process of assignment helps ensure that any differences between the groups at the end of the study can be attributed to the program and not to external factors, such as the motivation to apply. It is important to remember that, in this analysis, we estimate the average effect of the program on the whole treatment group whether students attended or not.

Throughout the study, we also gathered extensive data on program implementation, including summer attendance rates, how much academic time on task students received, and other features that varied across sites and classrooms. This information allowed us to conduct a set of correlational analyses that explore the relationship between implementation and outcomes. The volume and variety of data collected and analyzed through these different types of analyses provide readers with insights on how such programs can best be implemented, whether students will attend, whether students will benefit academically, and what factors appear most important in achieving good outcomes.

This study evaluates voluntary summer learning programs offered by five school districts, each varying by some key programmatic features, such as the specific academic curriculum and enrichment activities. Consequently, the study is a "proof of concept" of voluntary, district-led summer learning programs for low-income upper-elementary students, rather than an evaluation of the effectiveness of a particular program or curriculum in a specific locale. As a result, the findings should be particularly compelling for urban districts across the nation as they consider voluntary summer programming for low-income upper-elementary students.

Implementation Findings

Programs Implemented Common Features with Fidelity, but Instructional Quality Varied Within and Across Sites

Program leaders were diligent in implementing the common features requested of them in order to participate in this study. The programs were free and voluntary, with transportation and meals provided at no cost. Program leaders offered at least five weeks of programming with at least three scheduled hours of academics a day taught by certified teachers to small classes of students.

It is easier to determine fidelity to basic program features than to determine the quality of programming—we do not have objective measures of quality for all program features. We did see variation across and within sites as we observed students throughout each day. In each of the program sites, we observed challenges as well as several positive aspects of the programs. Typical instructional challenges included curricula that did not meet the academic needs of all students in the classroom and teachers not ensuring that all students understood the presented material. But in almost all of the classrooms we observed, teachers clearly communicated academic content to students who remained on task. The teachers reported that they enjoyed teaching in the programs, the sites were well managed, and logistics ran smoothly. Students had opportunities to participate in, and enjoyed, enrichment activities designed to be fun, and many students developed strong relationships with adults working in the programs.

Attendance Findings

One of the key contributions of this study is its detailed analysis of student attendance and its relationship with outcomes.

Participation Was Weaker in the Second Summer of the Study

Figure S.1 displays the attendance results for both summers, showing the proportion of treatment students in three groups: those who did not show up at all, those with relatively low attendance (attended from one to 19 days in one summer), and those who with relatively high attendance (20 days or more in one summer). We classified 20 or more days as "high" attendance based on a series of analyses to identify discrete cut points in the relationship between days of program attendance and students' outcomes.

About 20 percent of treatment students did not attend the summer program in 2013 and nearly half did not show up in the summer 2014 program. The 20-percent no-show rate in summer 2013 was lower than in 2011 and 2012, prior to the launch of the experiment, demonstrating that district actions can mitigate, although not eliminate, a no-show rate. Interestingly, we find no differences based on observable characteristics (e.g., achievement, race/ethnicity, family income) between students who did not show up (in either summer) and students who chose to attend. In summer 2014,

Figure S.1
Breakdown of Treatment Students' Attendance in Summers 2013 and 2014

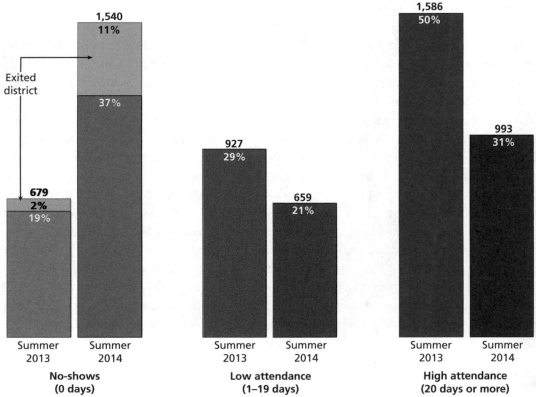

SOURCE: RAND analysis of districts' summer 2013 and 2014 attendance data.
NOTES: The numbers at the top of the bars are numbers of students in that category; percentages reflect proportion of the treatment group in that category.
RAND *RR1557-S.1*

the no-show rate sharply increased. To understand this spike, it is important to remember that it includes students who had left the district—about 11 percent of the total study sample. It also represents the nonparticipation rate of students who were invited 14 months earlier to attend the program in both summer 2013 and summer 2014. This time lag increased the possibility that students made other plans for the second summer. Because of this decline in participation from one summer to the next, both the low and high attenders in 2014 were a smaller proportion of the treatment group than in the first summer. That fact influenced our estimates of the impacts of the program on the treatment group.

Students Who Participated Attended an Average of About 75 Percent of the Time
Students who attended at least one day of the program in a given summer typically attended about 75 percent of the program days; remarkably, we observed this average

daily attendance rate in each of the four summers we studied. This average masks differences among districts, where average daily attendance ranged from a low of 60 percent to a high of 80 percent. Although districts with the lower rates made substantial efforts to improve attendance from 2011 (the year we began observing these programs) through 2014, their efforts did not have much effect.

We hypothesize that consistent summer attendance is inhibited by the following:

- a prevailing attitude that summer programs should be and are more relaxed than the school year, allowing for dropping in and out of the summer session
- the need for students to care for younger siblings at home
- changes to family plans and vacations
- student dislike of the program, which could be related to bullying or fighting among students
- competing opportunities, which could be related to observing activities of friends and neighbors (who were not in the program).

Of the students who attended at least one day, 60 percent were high attenders in each summer. This percentage varied by district, ranging from, in summer 2013, 52 percent of all attenders in one district to 85 percent in another. Across all the districts, we found that, compared with low attenders, high attenders had lower rates of eligibility for free or reduced-price meals, higher attendance rates during the prior school year, and higher prior achievement. The race/ethnicity makeup of the two attendance groups also differed, with the high-attendance group having a higher percentage of African Americans and Asians and fewer Hispanics than the low-attendance group.

Causal Findings on Program Effects

Our causal estimates compare the outcomes of all students who were randomly admitted to two summers of programming with the outcomes of all students who were randomly assigned to the control group, regardless of whether the students actually attended the summer program. As such, these estimates represent the impact of *offering* a summer learning program. Importantly, because many students who were offered the summer programs did not show up or had poor attendance, these estimates are expected to be smaller than the effects experienced by students who did attend regularly.

Modest Near-Term Benefit in Mathematics, Dissipated by the Next Fall

The first summer of programming resulted in a modest near-term benefit in mathematics measured in fall 2013, as shown in Figure S.2. The standardized average effect of offering the program was 0.08 and was statistically significant. As a point of comparison, researchers have concluded, based on studies of students the same age using

Figure S.2
Causal Effects of Summer Learning Programs on Measured Outcomes for All Treatment Group Students Relative to the Control Group Students

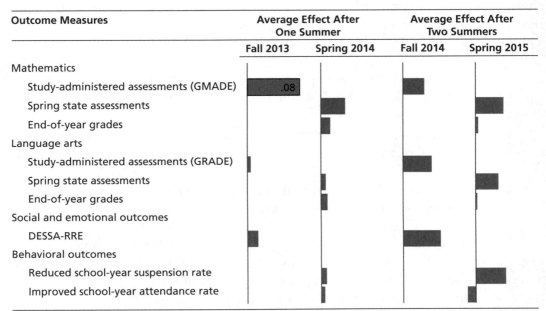

Outcome Measures	Average Effect After One Summer		Average Effect After Two Summers	
	Fall 2013	Spring 2014	Fall 2014	Spring 2015
Mathematics				
Study-administered assessments (GMADE)	.08			
Spring state assessments				
End-of-year grades				
Language arts				
Study-administered assessments (GRADE)				
Spring state assessments				
End-of-year grades				
Social and emotional outcomes				
DESSA-RRE				
Behavioral outcomes				
Reduced school-year suspension rate				
Improved school-year attendance rate				

NOTES: Horizontal length of the bar represents the magnitude of the program effect estimate, with the vertical line representing zero. Green indicates statistically significant after correction for multiple hypothesis tests. All models control for student baseline characteristics, including prior mathematics and English language arts (ELA) achievement, prior attendance and suspensions, poverty, race, gender, and classification as an English learner or a special education student. Blanks indicate data were not available for the particular outcome and time point. DESSA-RRE = Devereux Student Strengths Assessment–RAND Research Edition.
RAND *RR1557-S.2*

mathematics assessments similar to ours, that students have a 0.52 standardized effect size gain in mathematics from spring of one year to the following spring (Lipsey et al., 2012). By that benchmark, students in the treatment group experienced about 15 percent of that annual gain. A five-week summer program is about 10 percent of a calendar year and 15 percent of a school year. This benefit, however, did not show up in later assessments. Many studies conclude that the impacts of interventions fade over time.

We did not find near-term or longer-term benefits for any other outcomes we measured after that first summer. Nor did we find that some groups of students benefited more or less than others. English language learners, students eligible for free or reduced-price lunch, and students who had the lowest performance on prior achievement tests experienced approximately the same effects as other students in the treatment group.

No Causal Evidence That Two Summers of Programming Provided Benefits

When analyzing effects on all treatment students, we found no significant effects of offering two summers of programming for treatment students in mathematics, language arts, social-emotional competencies, or school-year behaviors. This result is not entirely surprising, given the fact that nearly half of the treatment students did not attend the program in the second summer. The students who did not attend in the second summer are still considered part of the treatment group in the causal analyses and as a result will dilute estimates of effects. The higher the no-show rate, the larger the effect of the program would have to be on those who do attend to be detected. For the same reason, if the effects accumulate in consecutive summers, they would have to accumulate by a substantial amount for us to be able to detect this trend statistically.

In spite of the low attendance rates across both summers, the causal results do show a pattern of positive effects across nearly all measures and time points, although the majority of these results are not statistically significant (except for mathematics performance after one summer). The consistency of these trends suggests that either the programs may confer some small benefits that could not be detected in this experiment or that the programs truly had minimal to no effect on the outcomes. We generally conclude that we have no evidence of causal impacts except for the near-term mathematics estimate after the first summer.

Correlational Findings on Program Effects

Our correlational analyses examine the relationship between certain implementation features and student participation rates to students' outcomes. These analyses are correlational (exploratory) rather than causal (experimental) because we are comparing all of the control group students with subsets of the treatment group that were not randomly determined. For that reason, selection bias remains a possibility, meaning that differences between the selected treatment subgroups and the control group in such pretreatment characteristics as achievement levels, family income, or English language learner status could explain differences in outcomes. To help mitigate the effects of potential selection bias, the outcome models for correlational analyses controlled for the same broad set of student characteristics as in our causal analyses, including student characteristics and prior academic performance. While we cannot rule out the possibility that unmeasured characteristics caused or contributed to the correlational results described below, we think the sum of evidence makes it likely that the academic results are due to participation in the summer learning programs. We are moderately less confident that the social-emotional results are not due to selection bias, because we lack a pretreatment measure of those outcomes for use as a statistical control.

Promising Evidence That High Attendance in One Summer Led to Mathematics Benefits Persisting Through the Following Spring

After summer 2013, students with high attendance received a near-term benefit in mathematics (0.13 or 25 percent of an average annual gain) that was also detected later on the spring 2014 state assessments (0.07 or 13 percent of the expected annual gain) (Lipsey et al., 2012). However, high attenders in 2013 did not receive a significant boost in language arts, social-emotional outcomes, or school-year behaviors (see Figure S.3). In each summer, about 60 percent of all students who attended at least one day were high attenders.

Promising Evidence That High Attendance in Second Summer Led to Mathematics and Language Arts Benefits That Persisted

For students who attended at high rates in summer 2014, we found positive near-term effects of the program in mathematics (0.11) and language arts (0.08) that were also demonstrated on state assessments in spring 2015 (0.14 and 0.09, respectively) (see Figure S.3). These represent between 20 percent and 25 percent of typical annual gains in mathemat-

Figure S.3
Correlational Effects of Program Attendance in Most Recent Summer on Assessment Outcomes on Subgroups of Treatment Group Students, Relative to the Control Group Students

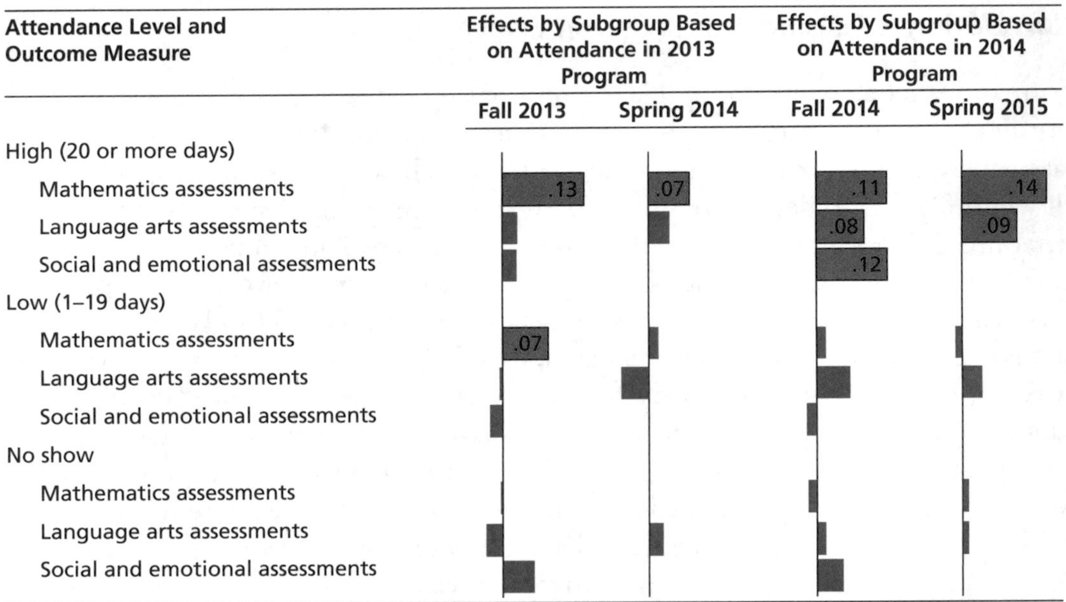

Attendance Level and Outcome Measure	Effects by Subgroup Based on Attendance in 2013 Program		Effects by Subgroup Based on Attendance in 2014 Program	
	Fall 2013	Spring 2014	Fall 2014	Spring 2015
High (20 or more days)				
Mathematics assessments	.13	.07	.11	.14
Language arts assessments			.08	.09
Social and emotional assessments			.12	
Low (1–19 days)				
Mathematics assessments	.07			
Language arts assessments				
Social and emotional assessments				
No show				
Mathematics assessments				
Language arts assessments				
Social and emotional assessments				

NOTES: Horizontal length of the bar represents the magnitude of the program effect estimate, with the vertical line representing zero. Green indicates statistically significant. All models control for student baseline characteristics, including prior mathematics and ELA achievement, prior attendance and suspensions, poverty, race, gender, and classification as an English learner or a special education student. Blanks indicate data were not available for the particular outcome and time point.
RAND RR1557-S.3

ics, and 20 percent and 23 percent of the typical annual gains in language arts for students at this age (Lipsey et al., 2012).[1] These positive outcomes most likely reflect a combination of cumulative program exposure and improved quality of programming in the second summer. Because the majority of high attenders in 2014 were also high attenders in 2013, we cannot determine whether the effects derive from cumulative attendance or from program improvements in the second summer (or both).

Promising Evidence That High Attendance in Second Summer Improved Social-Emotional Outcomes

We also found a positive benefit for high attenders in summer 2014 on the near-term measure of social-emotional competencies (for which we do not have a longer-term measure) (0.12). However, unlike the academic outcomes, for which we have pretreatment measures that we can use as controls in our models, we do not have a pretreatment measure of social-emotional competencies, so we are less confident that this estimate does not include bias.

Promising Evidence That High Levels of Academic Time on Task Led to Benefits That Persisted in Both Mathematics and Language Arts

Academic time on task was calculated by considering a student's attendance and our observations of the amount of time instructors spent on academic subjects. (In one district, for example, the plan was to provide 38 hours of language arts instruction over the summer, but classroom observations revealed that students received about 31 hours.) We found that students who received a minimum of about 25 hours of mathematics instruction or 34 hours in language arts in a given summer performed better on assessments in the relevant subject in fall 2013 (0.16 in mathematics and 0.05 in language arts) and fall 2014 (0.13 and 0.09) compared with students who received less instruction. For the sake of interpretation, the estimates represent between 23 percent and 31 percent of typical annual gains in mathematics, and between 14 percent and 23 percent of typical annual gains in language arts (Lipsey et al., 2012).

After the second summer, we also found that these positive effects persisted into the spring (0.11 in mathematics and 0.13 in language arts). About 35 percent of attending students experienced this level of academic time on task in mathematics and in language arts.

Promising Evidence That Students Who Received High-Quality Language Arts Instruction Benefited

We found consistent positive associations between the quality of instruction and language arts achievement. Our measure of quality focused on clear instruction, on-task

---

[1] Students at this grade have an average effect size gain from spring of one year to the following spring of 0.40 in language arts and 0.56 in mathematics (Lipsey et al., 2012).

behavior, and teachers ensuring that all students understood the material. The near-term effect of instructional quality, measured in fall 2013 after the first summer, was statistically significant. These positive trends persisted through the spring and fall 2014, although they were not significant.

Implications for Summer Program Leaders

Findings from this study should be generalizable to similar voluntary district-led programs offered at no cost to low-income late elementary urban students. Although the programs operated in specific contexts and were implemented by unique groups of administrators, teachers, and students, we have concluded that the results do not show evidence of meaningful variation in the effectiveness of the five programs. All five of the programs contributed toward the results.

This study provides evidence on what school districts and their community partners can expect if they commit to offering the kinds of programs we studied. For example, we demonstrate that the programs provided near-term benefits in mathematics after a single summer. The experimental evidence of these effects would be considered "strong" under the standards set forth in the new Every Student Succeeds Act (ESSA, Sec 8101 (21) (A)). Therefore, a summer learning program like those in this study might be eligible for federal funding under ESSA if the program targets mathematics skills.

We have also shown that high-attending students are likely to reap other benefits. These results are considered "promising" under ESSA, defined as "at least one well-designed and implemented correlational study that controls for selection bias," and districts might use them to demonstrate eligibility for federal funding if they can establish a track record of high attendance in their programs.

Beyond these outcomes, the detailed implementation analysis holds lessons for district leaders and other practitioners on how to improve the effectiveness of summer learning programs. Most of these lessons highlight the importance of maximizing the amount of instruction students receive over the summer:

Offer programs for at least five weeks. Given the finding that students who attended at least 20 days outperformed students who attended fewer days, and given the attendance rates we observed, programs with academic goals similar to the ones we studied should last at least five weeks—and ideally six or more weeks—with at least three hours of academics per day.

Create schedules that protect instructional time. Besides trying to maximize attendance, program leaders should protect time for academics by avoiding scheduled breaks and special activities during academic blocks. Protecting academic class time also entails building in realistic transition times between class periods and bathroom breaks throughout the day to ensure that classes do not start late, end early, or experience significant interruptions.

Track and maximize attendance rates. Because summer program attendance is critical to students' outcomes, we recommend that program leaders focus on it. However, we also recognize that the districts in the study strove to improve attendance each summer, with little success. Given what we have learned about the barriers to consistent attendance, we encourage districts to follow these practices:

- Offer programs to multiple grade levels to prevent older siblings from needing to care for younger children.
- Create engaging academic and enrichment opportunities that excite students.
- Employ adults who have time to focus on student behavior to minimize bullying and fighting among students.
- Make personal connections with families of students who may be more prone to low attendance (e,g., lower-achieving and lower-income students and students with poor school-year attendance) to encourage attendance of those students and to identify potential barriers to attendance.
- Establish mandatory programs for the lowest-performing students, who are less likely to attend the voluntary programs at high rates.

Invest in instructional quality. Focusing on instructional quality, particularly for language arts instruction, should benefit students in the summer (as it does during the school year). It can be challenging to ensure effective instruction in the summer. In programs like these, students attend a centralized summer site that is not typically their home school. Consequently, most teachers do not know the students, most students do not know one another, and there is a short time period to develop these relationships and create the kinds of classroom norms and routines that can support effective instruction. To minimize these challenges, program leaders are urged to take several steps:

- Recruit summer teachers with subject and grade-level experience who are often better able to connect the summer content to prior or upcoming school-year lessons. Our classroom observations suggest that despite small class sizes, not all teachers consistently checked for understanding and addressed misunderstandings when they arose.
- Encourage teachers to take the time to ensure that all students understand the academic material. Most teachers also found the summer curricula to be too advanced for the lowest-level learners, who made up about 40 percent of the sample.

- Provide teachers with a curriculum that aligns to the school year and state standards, while meeting the needs of the participating students, including low achievers.

Minimize costs by considering probable no-show and attendance rates. District leaders should examine their historical no-show and attendance rates when planning their programs. If they lack such data, the study suggests that they should expect a 20- to 30-percent no-show rate for a single voluntary summer program serving students in the upper-elementary grades. Districts should also expect that the students who participate will attend approximately 75 percent of the time. Districts can reduce their budget for summer programs (which, in this study, was estimated to be $1,340 per attending student) by using realistic projections to make decisions that are based on student numbers, such as determining how many teachers to hire and the amount of materials to order.

Acknowledgments

Many people helped in conducting this study and producing this report. We would like to thank those at The Wallace Foundation for their substantive and financial support. Ann Stone, Elizabeth Ty Wilde, Edward Pauly, and Lucas Held provided valuable guidance on the intellectual and analytic components of our work.

Representatives from the Boston, Dallas, Duval County, Pittsburgh, and Rochester summer programs generously allowed us access to observe their programs and to interview and survey stakeholders. We are particularly grateful to the people who allowed us to interview or observe them and to those who completed the surveys. Program materials and district data were provided when requested and we appreciate the time that goes into fulfilling those requests.

Several RAND staff members contributed to the data analyses and therefore to this report. Laura Zakaras helped us craft language that met the needs of both technical researchers and summer learning practitioners. Scott Naftel received, cleaned, and prepared all of the data we received from the districts. Courtney Ann Kase, Terry Marsh, Andrea Phillips, and Susannah Faxon-Mills observed instruction and collected survey data in the five districts; Geoffrey Grimm helped collect cost data. Stephanie Lonsinger and Sandy Petitjean assisted with editing and formatting. Former RAND staff contributed to this report as well. Paco Martorell at the University of California, Davis, had an early influence on the study design, and Daniel McCaffrey and J. R. Lockwood at the Educational Testing Service provided ongoing guidance on analytic approaches.

During the quality assurance and production process, Cathy Stasz provided valuable feedback on this document. Our peer reviewers, James Kim and Beth Ann Griffin, improved the quality of this report. Arwen Bicknell provided valuable editorial guidance.

Abbreviations

ADA	average daily attendance
DESSA-RRE	Devereux Student Strengths Assessment–RAND Research Edition
ELA	English language arts
ELL	English language learner
ESSA	Every Student Succeeds Act
GRADE	Group Reading Assessment and Diagnostic Evaluation
GMADE	Group Mathematics Assessment and Diagnostic Evaluation
ITT	intent to treat
NAEP	National Assessment of Educational Progress
NSLP	The National Summer Learning Project

CHAPTER ONE

Introduction

A persistent and substantial student achievement gap based on family income exists in the United States. On the National Assessment of Educational Progress (NAEP), 24 percent of fourth-grade students eligible for free or reduced-price lunch (an indicator of low family income) scored at or above the proficient level in mathematics, compared with 58 percent of students not eligible for the lunch program. Similar to this mathematics proficiency gap of 34 percentage points, the income achievement gap in reading is 31 percentage points (21 percent versus 52 percent scoring at least proficient). Since NAEP started tracking the income achievement gap in 2003, it has remained statistically unchanged. There are also large achievement gaps between white and black students, white and Hispanic students, and native speakers and English language learners (ELLs), and the gaps in performance persist into later grades (U.S. Department of Education, 2015).

These achievement gaps are likely to have substantial consequences for lifelong outcomes. Across the country, large disparities exist between students from low-income families and their peers from more-affluent families in terms of high school and college graduation rates. Only 70 percent of students from low-income families graduate from high school, compared with 85 percent of their more-affluent peers, and only 10 percent of individuals from lowest-income quartile families have a bachelor's degree by age 25, compared with 77 percent of individuals from families in the highest income quartile (National Center for Education Statistics, 2015; Pell Institute, 2015). Data from the U.S. Bureau of Labor Statistics (2014) show that individuals without a high school degree have unemployment rates that are 50 percent higher than high school graduates and 100 percent higher than college graduates. For individuals in the labor market, those with a bachelor's degree earn more than twice as much as high school graduates who, in turn, earn approximately 40 percent more than those without a high school diploma. In sum, the failure to reduce achievement gaps limits the economic mobility of children born into poverty.

Since the release of the influential Coleman report (Coleman et al., 1966), there has been an increased appreciation for the influence of students' out-of-school time on achievement and educational attainment and for the role these influences play in the development of persistent racial and socioeconomic achievement and attainment gaps. Even before students enter kindergarten, substantial achievement gaps exist along racial and socioeconomic lines (Reardon, Robinson-Cimpian, and Weathers, 2015).

Why Focus on Summer?

Summer vacation—which makes up about one-quarter of the calendar year—is another time when students face differential opportunities based on social and economic status of families. A seminal meta-analysis of summer learning (Cooper, Nye, et al., 1996) found that all students lost mathematics and reading knowledge over the summer, although the loss in mathematics knowledge was generally greater than in reading. This evidence also indicated that losses were larger for low-income students, particularly in reading.

While more-recent studies are inconclusive on the absolute loss of achievement over the summer, they provide additional evidence that low-income students experience setbacks over the summer relative to their wealthier peers (online Appendix C presents our literature review[1]). On average, most studies have found that low-income students learn less *relative* to their wealthier peers even if they do not experience *absolute* losses over the summer (Downey, Von Hippel, and Broh, 2004; McCoach et al., 2006; Benson and Borman, 2010; Ready, 2010; Von Hippel, Hamrock, and Kumar, 2016). This point is also supported in recent summer intervention evaluations (Kim, 2004; Benson and Borman, 2010; White et al., 2014). Likewise, students in low-income neighborhoods (Benson and Borman, 2010) and schools (White et al., 2014; Atteberry, McEachin, and Bloodworth, forthcoming) experienced larger losses over the summer relative to peers in wealthier neighborhoods or schools.

It is unclear what causes students of different backgrounds to have different summer achievement trajectories. Some research suggests that summer learning loss for low-income students could be related to students' opportunities to practice academic skills over the summer (Heyns, 1979; Cooper, Nye, et al., 1996; Downey, Von Hippel, and Broh, 2004). For example, Gershenson (2013) found that low-income students were more likely to watch two or more hours of television per day during the summer, on average, than were students from wealthier backgrounds.

Students from low-income families also have fewer opportunities for enriching nonacademic experiences relative to their peers from more-affluent families. For instance, approximately 59 percent of school-aged children from low-income families participate in sports, compared with 84 percent of children from wealthier families (those with annual incomes of $75,000 or more). These types of opportunity gaps exist for lessons and engagement in clubs as well (Pew Research Center, 2015).

---

[1]   Readers can find all detailed technical appendixes referred to in this report online at www.rand.org/pubs/research_reports/RR1557.

Summer programming is a potential mechanism to help improve outcomes for low-income and low-achieving students by providing additional instruction to struggling students, mitigating the differential effect that summer has on low-income students' achievement, and (for programs that also include enrichment activities) helping to bridge the income gap in such opportunities.

Indeed, prior research provides some evidence that summer programs can achieve some of these goals. Mandatory district-led programs and some small, voluntary programs operated primarily outside of districts have produced achievement gains for participants (Jacob and Lefgren, 2004; Borman, Benson, and Overman, 2005; Schacter and Jo, 2005; Chaplin and Capizzano, 2006; Matsudaira, 2008; Borman, Goetz, and Dowling, 2009; McCombs, Kirby, and Mariano, 2009). However, until this study, there has been little research evidence about the effectiveness of voluntary, district-led summer learning programs offered free of charge to large numbers of low-income and low-achieving students. In addition, the research literature provides little guidance on how to design and implement effective programs.

The National Summer Learning Project

In 2011, The Wallace Foundation initiated the National Summer Learning Project (NSLP) to expand summer opportunities for low-income students and to understand whether and how district-led voluntary summer learning programs that include academic instruction and enrichment opportunities can improve outcomes for low-income and low-achieving elementary school students. In spring 2011, The Foundation selected and began providing funding to support programs in five urban districts: Boston, Dallas, Duval County (Florida), Pittsburgh, and Rochester (New York). These districts already offered voluntary summer learning programs to low-income and low-achieving elementary school students and were willing to adopt common programming elements and participate in a randomized controlled trial for two summers. While districts made many programmatic design choices (e.g., in terms of curriculum) to fit district-specific needs, they enacted five common elements that characterize the NSLP model:

1. voluntary, full-day programming combining academics and enrichment for five days per week for no less than five weeks of the summer
2. at least three hours of instruction (language arts and mathematics) per day
3. small class sizes of no more than 15 students per adult
4. no fee to families for participation
5. free transportation and meals.

The common elements were selected in accordance with existing research and expert guidance. The programs also were designed to remove potential barriers to participation, such as cost and lack of transportation.

As part of this project, The Foundation also funded several technical assistance providers to support the program leaders with curriculum development, program planning, parent outreach, student recruitment, and other key functions. Also, program leaders were invited to join a professional learning community that convened members twice annually to share best practices and learn from them.

Programs at a Glance

Although the districts' programs shared key core characteristics, they also varied to reflect their local contexts (see Table 1.1). Two of the five districts operated their programs in partnership with local nonprofits. Two districts operated the program only for students in the studied grade (third grade in spring 2013), while the other three districts served multiple grade levels in each summer site. The structure of the day also differed across, and sometimes within, the districts. For instance, Pittsburgh's program offered academics in the morning and enrichment in the afternoon, while Duval's program interspersed academic and enrichment classes throughout the day. Enrichment offerings also differed across and sometimes within the programs. Each district also selected its own curriculum to use in language arts and mathematics. (A description of academic curricula is presented in Chapter Two.)

Phases of the Study

This study has been conducted in two phases: (1) a formative phase during which the selected programs worked on improvements to make them as strong as possible before the evaluation phase and (2) a summative evaluation phase including a randomized controlled trial implemented over two summers (2013 and 2014). We will track students' outcomes through spring 2017.

Phase I

In anticipation of the launch of the randomized controlled trial in spring 2013, The Wallace Foundation first funded two preparatory years in each of the five school districts. Specifically, for summers 2011 and 2012, The Foundation partially funded the summer programs, including programmatic expansion and improvement, curricular consultants, peer collaboration, and external formative evaluation. The RAND Corporation conducted formative evaluations of program implementation in each district in summers 2011 and 2012, providing feedback and recommendations to the districts each fall. In addition, we published our analysis of summer 2011 data in *Getting to Work on Summer Learning: Recommended Practices for Success* (Augustine et al., 2013), which provides advice for planning and implementing summer programs.

Table 1.1
Summer 2014 Program Characteristics

Characteristic	Boston	Dallas	Duval	Pittsburgh	Rochester
Name of summer program	Summer Learning Project	Thriving Minds Summer Camp	Super Summer Academy	Summer Dreamers Academy	Rochester Summer Scholars
Program leader(s)	Boston After School and Beyond with Boston Public Schools	Dallas Independent School District with Big Thought	Duval County Public Schools	Pittsburgh Public Schools	Rochester City School District
Summer sites serving students in the study	10	8	8	3	1, organized into 3 "houses"
Program served other grades	No	Yes	Yes	Yes	No
Job titles of adults managing the sites	• Site coordinator (public school employee) • Community-based organization representatives	• Principal • Assistant principal • Big Thought site manager • Counselor • Data clerk • Office manager	• Principal • Assistant principal • Counselor • Data clerk	• Director • Behavior coach • Curriculum coaches • Activity director • Operations managers • Special-education teachers	• Principal • Assistant principals • Site coordinators • Behavior specialists • Curriculum coaches • Special-education consultants • Bilingual consultants • Social worker
Duration (days)	25–30	24	29	25	25
Daily hours	Varied: typically seven-hour days	8:00 a.m.–4:00 p.m.	8:15 a.m.–3:45 p.m.	8:30 a.m.–4:00 p.m.	7:30 a.m.–3:30 p.m.
Program structure	Varied by site. Typically academics in the morning and enrichment in the afternoon	Academics in the morning, enrichment in the afternoon	Students rotated through sections of academics and enrichment throughout the day	Academics in the morning, enrichment in the afternoon	Academics in the morning, enrichment in the afternoons. Writing offered during the afternoons as well
Enrichment activities	Varied by site: • Tennis • Sailing • Nature walks • Ropes course • Archery • Arts and crafts • Swimming • Boat building	Varied by site: • Dance • Music • Physical education • Theater • Visual arts	Varied by site: • Dance • Music • Physical education • Theater • Visual arts • Arts and crafts	Varied by site: • Fencing • Music • Science • Visual arts • Water polo	Varied by site: • Cooking • Dance • Rock climbing • Sand sports • Swimming

For some districts, the formative feedback led to program improvements year after year. For example, districts started their summer program planning processes earlier, improved logistics (such as transportation), and revamped summer school curricula to better align with the school year. However, this was not the case in each district. Also, some districts faced challenges that were not overcome—for instance, despite their efforts, districts were unable to substantially improve attendance rates over time.

Phase II

The second phase of the study started in spring 2013. During this phase, the activities of Phase I continued (Wallace financial support, peer learning, curricular support, formative evaluation) and the randomized controlled trial began. A randomized controlled trial is a rigorous experiment that, in this case, randomly assigned students who applied to the summer program into two groups: a treatment group that had the opportunity to participate in two consecutive summers of programming and a control group that did not. The focus of the randomized controlled trial was on the cohort of third-graders in spring 2013 (see online Appendix A for details on randomization design and implementation). This lottery-like process, which resulted in statistically equivalent groups, assures that any differences between the groups at the end of the study can be attributed to the program and not to external factors, such as motivation to apply for the summer program.

After districts recruited third-graders for the program in spring 2013, RAND randomized applicants into the two groups (treatment and control) in each of the five districts. Students assigned to the treatment group were accepted into the program for both summer 2013 and 2014. Students assigned to the control group were not admitted to the program for either of those two summers but were provided with lists of free nonacademic summer programs in their community. In one district, control group families were provided with a stipend to help defray the cost of other summer programs.

Throughout Phase II, we continued collecting implementation data: We gathered detailed summer attendance data, surveyed all summer teachers, interviewed summer teachers and site coordinators, and observed each classroom of students for an entire day in both summers. (For details on this part of the study, see online Appendix B.) We used these implementation data in our descriptive and correlational analyses and to provide the districts with feedback each fall in an effort to continue strengthening their programs.

We also collected student outcomes data at multiple points in time—fall 2013, spring 2014, fall 2014, spring 2015—and we will continue to track outcomes through spring 2017.

Students in the Study

McCombs, Pane, et al. (2014) describes the process for setting eligibility criteria for students in the study, recruiting these students, and randomly assigning them to the treatment or control group. Districts were asked *not* to recruit any students for the study who were required to attend a summer program because of poor grades or the threat of grade retention. These students were allowed to attend the programs we studied (or other programs offered in the districts) but were not eligible to participate in the study because they could not be randomized into the control group.

In 2013, demand for the programs was strong across the five districts— 5,639 eligible third-grade students applied, exceeding recruitment goals in all districts. The number of students in the study varied by district (Table 1.2). In April and May 2013, we randomized students in each district. Across the districts, more than 3,000 students were assigned to the treatment group (57 percent), and 2,445 (43 percent) were assigned to the control group. We assigned the larger percentage of students to the treatment group in an effort to balance the desire to admit as many students as possible with the need to retain sufficient statistical power. As expected from a random selection process, characteristics are very similar between the treatment and control groups (see online Appendix B for further detail).

As shown in Table 1.2, the students who participated in the study were largely nonwhite and low income. Across the districts, 47 percent of students in the study were African-American and 40 percent were Hispanic. Eighty-nine percent were eligible for free or reduced-price lunch, an indicator of low family income. Overall, 31 percent of students in the study had ELL status; Dallas had the highest proportion at 59 percent.

Table 1.2
Demographic Profile of All Students in the Study, by District

District	Students in the Study	African American (%)	Hispanic (%)	Asian (%)	White (%)	FRPL (%)	ELL (%)	Lowest Achieving[a] (%)	IEP (%)
Boston	957	42	41	6	8	NA	30	24	15
Dallas	2,056	19	77	1	1	95	59	43	5
Duval	888	79	5	1	12	87	3	12	8
Pittsburgh	656	70	3	3	17	83	7	39	17
Rochester	1,080	65	22	4	8	82	16	81	15
Total	**5,637[b]**	**47**	**40**	**3**	**7**	**89**	**31**	**42**	**10**

SOURCE: District student-level data from school year 2012–2013.

NOTES: Racial and ethnic categories may not add to 100 percent since "other" is not shown.
FRPL = students eligible for free or reduced-price lunch; IEP = students with individualized education plans (special education).

[a] *Lowest achieving* is defined as students scoring at the lowest proficiency level on either the spring 2013 mathematics or reading state tests.

[b] Two students initially randomized are not represented in this table because of withdrawal of parental consent to use the students' data for this study.

Across the districts, 10 percent of students had special-education needs, as indicated by having an individualized education plan, ranging from 5 percent in Dallas to 17 percent in Pittsburgh.

In addition, approximately 42 percent of students in the study had scored at the lowest level of proficiency in language arts, mathematics, or both on their statewide standardized spring 2013 assessments. However, there was wide variation at the district level, ranging from a low of 12 percent of students in Duval to a high of 81 percent of students in Rochester. This variation may be partly because of the varying difficulty of tests from state to state or to the different cut points that states use to assign students to proficiency levels, but it also reflects district policies that affected student eligibility for the program. In Duval, for example, students scoring at the lowest level on the state reading assessment were mandated to attend a separate summer program and were thus not eligible to participate in the study.

Research Questions and Publications

This study was designed to answer several research questions:

1. How well are the programs implemented, including site management, quality of academic and enrichment instruction, time spent on academic instruction, site culture, and cost?
2. What is student participation in one summer and two summers of programming?
3. What is the effect of admission to one summer of voluntary summer programming on student achievement, behavior, and social-emotional outcomes, measured in the fall and spring after that summer?
4. What is the effect of admission to two consecutive summers of voluntary summer programming on student achievement, behavior, and social-emotional outcomes, measured in the fall and spring after the second summer?
5. Do student characteristics—such as achievement level, family income, or ELL status—moderate outcomes?
6. What factors, including program implementation and student attendance, influence student outcomes?

The study is producing a series of public reports with insights for the field on effectiveness and implementation. The first report, *Getting to Work on Summer Learning: Recommended Practices for Success* (Augustine et al., 2013) provided guidance on program implementation and operations. The second report, *Ready for Fall? Near-Term Effects of Voluntary Summer Learning Programs on Low-Income Students' Learning Opportunities and Outcomes* (McCombs et al., 2014), reported on near-term student outcomes after one summer of programming. This report, the third in the series, shares findings on implementation and outcomes after two summers of programming, addressing all of our research questions. A subsequent report will examine student outcomes through spring 2017, two years after summer 2014 programming. Consequently, our understanding of the effects of these programs on student outcomes will develop further as we collect additional data for analysis. In addition, we will publish another report in 2017 on operational lessons and guidance for running summer programs based on the districts' experiences in summers 2011–2014.

We are also conducting a related set of studies that examine how summer breaks influence students' learning trajectories, the policy context for summer programming, and the integration of summer programming and planning into districts' and communities' objectives and activities. These studies will be published over the next few years.

Contributions of This Multifaceted, Longitudinal Research Approach

This study of summer learning programs is unique in its scope, length, and analytic rigor. In terms of scope, it is the broadest study of its kind. It includes five large school districts across the country; it examines many potential program outcomes in the analysis; and it includes an analysis of program implementation and its relationship with those outcomes. It is also the longest study of its kind, beginning in 2011 and concluding in 2017, tracking outcomes for four years after students entered the summer programs. Because it includes a randomized controlled trial design, the experimental results provide strong evidence on whether summer programs boost students' academic and behavioral outcomes. Throughout the study, we have also gathered extensive data regarding program implementation, including attendance, which allows us to conduct a rigorous set of correlational analyses that explore the relationship between implementation and outcomes. The volume and variety of data collected and analyzed provide insights on voluntary summer learning programs targeted to low-income youth—how they can best be implemented, whether students will attend, whether students will benefit academically, and what factors appear most important in achieving good outcomes.

We offer more detail about each of these contributions in this section. More details about our data collection activities, instruments, and methods can be found in online Appendix B.

Five Urban Districts

The study evaluates voluntary summer learning programs in five different urban contexts, each varying by some key programmatic features (such as the specific academic curriculum and enrichment activities). As such, this study is a "proof of concept" of voluntary, district-led summer learning programs for low-income upper-elementary students, rather than an evaluation of the effectiveness of a particular program or curriculum in a specific locale. This being the case, the findings should be particularly compelling for urban district leaders across the nation as they consider voluntary summer programming for low-income upper-elementary students.

Multiple Outcomes

The study investigates multiple outcome measures, including academic achievement in language arts and mathematics, social-emotional outcomes, and school-year attendance and suspensions.

Specifically, we examine:

- fall 2013 and fall 2014 academic achievement in language arts and mathematics, measured using a broad, generalized, standardized assessment (Group Reading Assessment and Diagnostic Evaluation [GRADE]/Group Mathematics Assessment and Diagnostic Evaluation [GMADE])[2]
- fall 2013 and fall 2014 social-emotional status, using a validated teacher-report instrument on student competencies (Devereux Student Strengths Assessment–RAND Research Edition [DESSA-RRE])
- spring 2014 and spring 2015 academic achievement in language arts and mathematics, measured by state assessments
- school years 2013–2014 and 2014–2015 course grades in language arts and mathematics
- school-year suspensions in 2013–2014 and 2014–2015
- school-year attendance in 2013–2014 and 2014–2015.

Reporting Outcomes

In examining the effects of the summer programs on these student outcomes, we follow customary procedure in the education research community by reporting standardized effect sizes to quantify the difference between the treatment and control groups.[3] By using standardized effect sizes, we can compare the magnitude of program effects across the various outcome measures. For example, we use effect sizes to examine whether the programs have a larger impact on language arts or mathematics outcomes. Standardization also allows us to compare program effects from these programs with others. Despite the standardization, we caution that the magnitude of an effect size is influenced by a number of factors—including the type of assessment used, grade level and subject, and type of study conducted—

---

[2]   These assessments were selected because they are broad, general-knowledge, standardized assessments at an appropriate level of difficulty for the study population. Additional detail regarding the assessments can be found in the technical appendix.

[3]   An *effect size* quantifies the difference between two groups. We report effect sizes in standardized units, which are expressed as a fraction of the standard deviation (or spread) of the post-test scores. We also use effect sizes to report the differences between segments of the treatment group (e.g., students with high attendance rates) and the control group in our correlational analyses.

which must be considered when comparing effect sizes found in this report to effect sizes from other studies.

In particular, it may be useful to consider the following data—all shown in standardized effect size units—to help set realistic benchmarks for what effect sizes to expect in this study.

- Annual spring-to-spring gains on broad standardized assessments vary by subject and grade level, from as large as 1.52 in reading between spring of kindergarten and spring of first grade, to as small as 0.01 in mathematics from spring of 11th grade to spring of 12th grade (Lipsey et al., 2012). In general, annual gains in effect size are larger in mathematics than in reading and decline as students age. For the grade span covered by the study to date (spring of third grade to spring of fifth grade), the averages are annual gains of 0.38 in reading and 0.54 in mathematics. A five-to-six week summer program represents 10 percent of a calendar year and 15 percent of a school year, so the effects of those programs would likely be correspondingly smaller.
- Among randomized controlled trial studies of elementary schools, mean effect sizes have been largest (0.40) when the outcome is measured by specialized tests, such a researcher-developed or curriculum-based assessments, and smallest (0.08) when measured by broadly focused standardized tests, such as those used in the study (Lipsey et al., 2012).
- A recent meta-analysis of education studies found that large, randomized controlled trial studies like ours measured average effects of 0.11 (Cheung and Slavin, 2016).

Combining these observations, we conclude that it is realistic to expect effect sizes in this study to be in the range of 0.10 or smaller—indeed, we powered the study to be able to detect effects of about this magnitude. Effects of this magnitude appear likely to be educationally meaningful when benchmarked against typical spring-to-spring gains, particularly if they persist.

Longitudinal Treatment and Outcome Measurement

The longitudinal nature of the study is a key strength. We have data on the same outcomes of interest at multiple time points; this allows us to investigate persistence of effects from the near term into the long term and further allows us to investigate the effect of two summers of programming. For example, when we examine whether offering the summer program has an impact on student achievement, we estimate the impact of:

- one summer on fall achievement (fall 2013)
- one summer on spring achievement (spring 2014)
- two summers on fall achievement (fall 2014)
- two summers on spring achievement (spring 2015).

One implication of the study's design is that we are unable to experimentally examine the impact of one summer of programming beyond spring 2014. Also, we are unable to experimentally examine the impact of the second summer alone.

To facilitate the interpretation of the findings and trends across years, we summarize the findings through charts and present details in online Appendix F. Also, we are mindful as we make recommendations that our knowledge about the effectiveness of the programming is likely to improve as more years of data become available.

Analytic Techniques and Strength of Evidence

We conducted a rigorous set of analyses—descriptive, confirmatory causal, and exploratory correlational—to address our research questions. Table 1.3 lists those questions, the type of analysis used to examine them, and the strength of evidence that each type of analysis produces, as specified by the Every Student Succeeds Act (ESSA).[4] (For more detail on our research approach, see online Appendix E.)

Descriptive Analyses

The first two research questions require descriptive analyses. Many randomized controlled trials are criticized because they provide strong evidence of outcomes but lack

Table 1.3
Analytic Category and Evidence Rating of the Study's Research Questions

Research Question	Analytic Category	Evidence Rating Under ESSA*
How well are the programs implemented, including site management, quality of academic and enrichment instruction, instructional time on task, site culture, and cost?	Descriptive	N/A
What is student participation in one summer and two summers of programming?	Descriptive	N/A
What is the effect of admission of one summer of voluntary summer programming on student achievement and social-emotional outcomes, measured in the fall and spring after that summer?	Confirmatory Causal	Strong
What is the effect of admission to two consecutive summers of voluntary summer programming on student achievement and social-emotional outcomes, measured in the fall and spring after the second summer?	Confirmatory Causal	Strong
Do student characteristics—such as achievement level, family income, or ELL status—moderate outcomes?	Confirmatory Causal	Strong
What factors, including program implementation and student attendance, influence student outcomes?	Exploratory Correlational	Promising

---

[4]   ESSA defines four levels of evidence: (1) strong evidence as emerging from at least one well-designed and well-implemented experimental study, (2) moderate evidence from at least one well-designed and well-implemented quasi-experimental study, (3) promising evidence from at least one well-designed and well-implemented correlational study with statistical controls for selection bias, and (4) programs with a rationale based on high-quality research or a positive evaluation that suggests it is likely to improve student or other relevant outcomes.

information on how these outcomes were (or were not) achieved. This study was intentionally designed to look inside the "black box" to provide descriptive data on implementation, including attendance.

Our program implementation findings are based on the following:

- **Attendance data from administrative records on all students in the study.** The study team worked with the districts and monitored summer attendance-taking practices during the study, which increases our confidence in the validity of these data.
- **Daylong observations of classroom cohorts of students, meaning groups of students who remained together throughout the day.** Each day, we selected one cohort and followed them the entire day, noting many aspects of their experiences, including detailed observations of academic and enrichment classes. This process yielded 783 classroom observations in summer 2013 and 608 in summer 2014 and covered about 10 percent of the total number of language arts and mathematics classes that occurred over the two summers.
- **A daily site-climate survey completed by our field researchers in summer 2014.** At the end of each full day at a summer site, observers recorded aspects of site climate, with a particular focus on staff-to-student and student-to-student interactions. In total, we conducted 154 of these site-climate observations in summer 2014; they were spread across the 34 total summer sites within the five school districts.
- **A survey of all mathematics and language arts summer teachers,** with a 95-percent response rate in summer 2013 and 98-percent response rate in summer 2014.
- **Interviews with more than 75 teachers and site administrators.**
- **Program documents,** including daily schedules and curricular documents from each summer, reports submitted by technical assistance providers, and minutes from ongoing program teleconferences.
- **Cost data obtained from districts for summer 2014.**
- **Survey of all students** in the study in fall 2013 and fall 2014 to gather information on their activities during the summer.

Causal Analyses

Research questions 3, 4, and 5 about program effectiveness are answered using causal analyses that compare outcomes of treatment and control students. A randomized controlled trial is the most rigorous method of causal analysis because the lottery-like process of assigning students to the two groups helps ensure that any differences between the groups at the end of the study can be attributed to the program and not to external factors, such as motivation to apply for the summer program. The program effects estimated in these analyses are the effects of *offering* the program to students—that is, the average effect of the program on all treatment students admitted to the program, including those who did not participate. Figure 1.1 illustrates that process.

Figure 1.1
Causal Analyses Compare Outcomes for All Treatment and Control Group Students

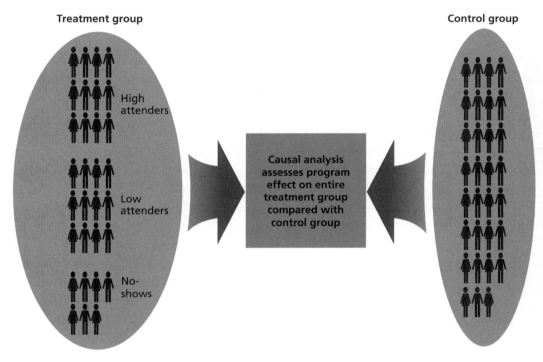

Because the study tests many hypotheses about the effects of summer programs (we have multiple outcomes at multiple time periods), we adjusted our estimates of statistical significance to guard against finding spurious significant effects. This correction has become more common over the past decade and is considered best practice, but it does deviate from older studies, which did not make this correction and may have found statistically significant effects that would not be significant with such adjustment. Our causal analyses produce "strong evidence" under the definitions of levels of evidence provided by ESSA and meet the highest level of evidence under What Works Clearinghouse standards (U.S. Department of Education, 2014).

Correlational Analyses

The final research question, which examines what program features or levels of student participation are related to outcomes, is of particular interest to practitioners because it provides guidance on implementation. We illuminate these relationships through correlational analyses. As illustrated in Figure 1.2, this type of analysis compares the performance of certain subgroups, rather than the entire treatment group, to the control group as a whole. Since these students were not randomly assigned to these subgroups,

Figure 1.2

Correlational Analyses Estimate Program Effects for Subsets of the Treatment Group

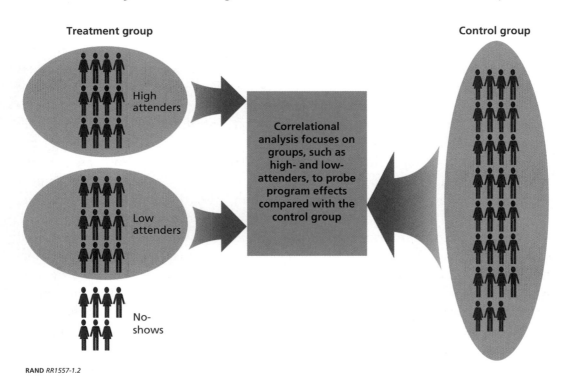

RAND *RR1557-1.2*

we cannot assume they have the same observed and unobserved characteristics as the control group.

To reduce the chance of bias in these analyses, we used a rich set of student background variables (including prior achievement) as statistical controls, but we cannot control for unmeasured differences (such as parental support or students' motivation to learn), which could bias our estimates of program effects for these groups of interest. Results from these analyses rate as promising under ESSA.[5] They complement results of our causal analyses and shed light on the relationship between implementation, including attendance, and student outcomes.

Study Limitations

This evaluation is most relevant for summer programs with the features we have described; there are other types of summer learning programs (e.g., school-based

---

[5]   To make the text flow more naturally, we do not identify the limitations of the correlational analyses in every sentence. As such, our use of terms such as "boost," "effects," and "benefits" when describing correlational findings are not intended to indicate that a causal link has been established.

programs offered to students who attend that same school during the year, mandatory programs, or those focused on only one academic subject) to which the findings are unlikely to generalize. For example, the average daily attendance (ADA) in the voluntary summer programs we studied was substantially lower than attendance in mandatory summer programs. These findings are also less likely to generalize to other age groups, such as children in the earliest elementary grades or high-school students.

Despite the study's scope, it does not address all questions of potential interest. For example, we do not measure how much of the intended content that students learned during the summer. In the study, we rely on generalized assessments of achievement to understand whether summer programs broadly affect students' language arts and mathematics performance, rather than on curriculum-based pre/post assessments, which are specialized tests used to answer questions about how much intended content students learned from specific summer curriculum. Also, the study does not measure summer learning loss. Students did not take the same test in spring and again in fall, so we do not know if students who did not attend the summer program experienced summer slide or held steady in their mathematics or language arts skills by the time they returned to school in the fall. Instead, we compare the outcomes of students who were admitted to the programs with those who were not, with statistical adjustment for student performance and other characteristics measured before the start of the study.

Our measure of social-emotional outcomes is a valid measure of self-motivation and self-regulation; however, it is limited to teacher perceptions of student behavior. It does not measure student aspiration, sense of self-efficacy, attachment to school, or other potentially important attributes.

There are benefits of these programs that may have affected students in ways that we do not capture. For example, the programs provided many students with opportunities they may not have had otherwise, such as to swim, rock climb, cook, and experience new environments. In one district, we heard students comment that they had never before left the city to visit a nature preserve, walk in the woods, or take a boat to an island. Programs also provided students with meals—both breakfast and lunch—and some even provided students with a snack or dinner to take home for the evening. In another district, we observed program leaders providing needed clothing to students. In yet another, a social worker organized a "girls' breakfast" and a "girls' lunch" to bring rising fifth-graders together in small groups to talk about their interpersonal relationships. We do not have good measures of how these aspects of the programs might have influenced students and their families.

Finally, the study was not designed to have sufficient statistical power to detect effects within districts nor to detect differential district contributions to the overall results. Nonetheless, we explored these questions and concluded that we do not have evidence that districts had differential contributions toward any of the results we highlight in these chapters.

Report Overview

This report draws upon longitudinal data through spring 2015 and examines the implementation and effectiveness of voluntary summer learning programming for low-income students in five school districts. We chose to mask the identities of the districts in tables and figures; we use the labels District A through District E, but these designations do not consistently identify the same district across the tables and chapters.

The remainder of this report is presented in five chapters. Chapter Two describes program implementation in the five districts. Chapter Three analyzes student attendance in the summer programs. Chapters Four and Five present causal and correlational results from fall 2013 through spring 2015. Chapter Six closes the report with our conclusions.

As already noted, readers can find the detailed technical appendixes referred to in this report online at www.rand.org/pubs/research_reports/RR1557. Appendix A describes the randomization design and implementation, Appendix B describes the data collection undertaken in this study, Appendix C presents an updated literature review on summer learning loss and summer program effectiveness, Appendix D discusses the construction of variables measuring hypothesized mediators of summer program effects, Appendix E describes details of the statistical analyses we conducted, and Appendix F contains the results of all the regression models, whether or not discussed in this report.

CHAPTER TWO

Summer Programs in Practice: Implementation Findings

In this chapter, we describe how the summer programs were enacted. The purpose of this chapter is twofold: to provide context and to describe how we measured implementation features that we further examine in Chapter Five. To understand implementation, we describe academic instruction, enrichment provision, summer sites' climate, program revenue, and program costs. Within these sections, we describe how we measured these programmatic aspects. In addition to students' attendance patterns, which are described in Chapter Three, the implementation features we further analyze in Chapter Five include the following:

- teacher's prior teaching experiences with the sending or receiving grade level
- alignment of the curriculum to students' needs
- quality of instruction in students' mathematics and language arts classrooms
- amount of academic time on task a student received
- relative opportunity for individual attention, which combines academic time on task and class size
- positive instructional climate
- site discipline and order
- daily site climate.

In summary, program leaders effectively implemented the common features required for study inclusion. The programs were free and voluntary, with transportation and healthy meals provided at no cost. There were at least five weeks of programming with at least three scheduled hours of academics a day taught by certified teachers to small classes of students. It is easier to determine fidelity to these basic program features than to determine the quality of programming. Although we describe strengths as well as challenges facing the summer programs, we do not have objective measures of quality for all program features.

Academic Instruction

To illuminate academic instruction, we describe the summer teachers, the curriculum they used, their instruction of this curriculum, and the amount of time on task spent in both language arts and mathematics. In both summers, students generally remained on task as they learned in small classes ranging, by district, from an average of eight to 13 students per adult in the classroom. Teachers reported high levels of satisfaction with their summer position and in interviews cited the benefits of the small class sizes. In Chapter Five, we examine the link between class size and minutes of instruction and students' outcomes.

Teachers

Compared with the regular school year, teachers have a very short time period during the summer to impart content to students. For this reason, best practice encourages maximizing the match between teacher grade level and content experience and their summer teaching assignment (McCombs, Pane, et al., 2014). Ideally, the summer academic teachers are those who teach the same subject and either the sending or receiving grade level of students (that is, the grade level that students are either leaving before summer begins or entering when summer is over). These teachers are well versed in the school-year curriculum that the summer students either just completed or are about to receive and can thus connect the summer content to the most important, or most frequently skipped or misunderstood, concepts from the school year.

Table 2.1 shows how districts varied in their ability to implement this match. In 2013, 61 percent of teachers had taught the sending or receiving grade, 86 percent of math teachers had taught math, and 87 percent of language arts teachers had taught language arts in the prior school year. These matches worsened in 2014, when 53 percent of teachers had taught the sending or receiving grade, 61 percent of math teachers had taught math, and 66 percent of language arts teachers had taught language arts in the prior school year. These matches also varied by district. In 2014, for example, only 27 percent of summer teachers in one district had taught either fourth or fifth grade during the prior school year, while 83 percent of teachers had done so in another district. Similarly, only 21 percent of mathematics teachers had taught mathematics in the prior school year in one district—although 100 percent of mathematics teachers had taught that subject in another district. In language arts, 50 percent of teachers had taught the subject during the prior school year in one district, and, at the high end, 88 percent of summer language arts teachers had taught that subject during the prior school year. In Chapter Five, we explore whether teachers' backgrounds are related to student outcomes.

It is unclear why some districts had more success in hiring teachers with grade or subject matches than others. We hypothesize that local teacher labor markets, competing summer programs, and program reputation may influence teacher applications. In addition, at least one district prioritized attracting the same teachers in 2014 who had taught the study cohort in 2013. This choice worsened the grade-level match between

Table 2.1
Qualifications of Summer Program Academic Teachers by District, Summers 2013 and 2014

Qualification	2013	2014
Taught either fourth or fifth grade in 2013–2014 school year (%)	61	53
Summer mathematics teachers who also taught math in 2013–2014 school year (%)	86	61
Summer language arts teachers who also taught language arts in 2013–2014 school year (%)	87	66

SOURCES: RAND data collected from teachers or districts about summer 2014 teachers.

summer 2013 and 2014, while at the same time might have benefited students who already had a relationship with a particular teacher. In one district that had more success in hiring teachers with a grade and subject match, the program leaders, rather than the summer site principals, selected the teachers. Perhaps because hiring decisions were centralized and because the program leaders valued hiring teachers with aligned grade-level and subject-matter backgrounds, they were more successful in this regard.

Summer Curricula

In selecting a curriculum for the summer program, district leaders needed to balance grade level standards with student skills and knowledge levels. Those levels varied, as demonstrated in Table 2.2. In most of the districts, the majority of students had scored at the basic level or below on the English language arts (ELA) state assessments. Students had performed slightly better on the mathematics assessments. Students' prior

Table 2.2
Percentages of Students in the Study at Given Performance Levels Based on Spring 2013 State Assessments

	District A	District B	District C	District D	District E
Level 1					
ELA	14	24	0	37	73
Math	19	35	12	17	69
Level 2					
ELA	56	57	50	16	21
Math	33	55	31	27	24
Level 3					
ELA	27	19	26	39	5
Math	34	10	37	37	5
Level 4					
ELA	2	NA	19	8	0
Math	14	NA	15	20	1
Level 5					
ELA	NA	NA	5	NA	NA
Math	NA	NA	5	NA	NA

NA = not applicable.

achievement levels varied by district, reflecting, at least in part, decisions about which students to target for the summer program under study.

Table 2.3 presents the curricula that districts used for language arts and mathematics in summer 2014. The mathematics curricula tended to focus on fractions and decimals and review of multiplication and division. Although each of the language arts curriculum included a focus on reading nonfiction informational texts, most incorporated several activities, such as vocabulary, writing, and phonics lessons, as well as independent reading activities and group work. Most of the districts used the same curriculum in both summers, adjusting for the higher grade level. However, two selected a new language arts curriculum in summer 2014 to better align with their state's standards.

In both 2013 and 2014, by the first day of the summer programs, the vast majority of teachers had received the language arts and mathematics curricula, including pacing guides and lesson plans.[1] On our survey, most of the teachers reported that the cur-

Table 2.3
Curricula Used in Summer 2014 for the Rising Fifth-Grade Cohort

District	Mathematics	Language Arts
A	• Number Worlds Level G Fifth Grade • District-selected math "read aloud" and math games • District-developed "Problem of the Week"	• National Geographic's Language, Literacy, and Vocabulary—Reading Expeditions: Social Studies and Science • Syllasearch • Novel study
B	• Voyager Summer Math Adventure: Decimals and Fractions • CCSS New York State Fractions Module • District-developed daily computational fluency routines	• American Reading Company: Ecosystems: Reading and Writing Informational Text • Phonics Blitz/Phonics Boost or Novel Study
C	• Voyager Summer Math Adventure: Grade 4/Level E Modules 3–6 • District-developed problem exemplars and games • District-developed "number of the day" routine	• National Geographic's Language, Literacy, and Vocabulary—Reading Expeditions: Social Studies • District-developed read aloud • District-developed writing workshop
D	• Voyager Summer Math Adventure: Grade 4/Level E Modules 1–6 • District-developed performance based tasks and games	• American Reading Company Summer Semester: reading and writing informational texts
E	• Summer Success Math	• National Geographic's Language, Literacy, and Vocabulary—Reading Expeditions: Social Studies • Achieve 3000 • Good Reader Guide • USA Weekly Reader • District-developed weekly culminating independent project

SOURCES: RAND data collected from districts.

---

[1] This information is based on the RAND survey of academic teachers. See online Appendix B for a sample of the survey instrument.

ricular materials were clear and the pacing was reasonable. In 2014, with one exception (teachers in one district did not think that the mathematics curriculum was aligned to the next grade level's standards), at least 70 percent of the teachers who had taught either the sending or the receiving grade in the prior school year found the curriculum to be aligned to both the prior school year and the upcoming school year curriculum in both mathematics and reading. However, few teachers received or had examined data on the students from the prior school year to help them with planning and differentiating their instruction.

In both summers, most teachers believed that their students' mathematics and reading skills improved over the summer; nevertheless, teachers' responses to other survey questions about the curricula highlight how challenging it is to select a summer curriculum that addresses all participating students' ability levels. Figures 2.1 and 2.2 demonstrate this point. Although most 2014 teachers found the curriculum to be a strong match for students who generally received basic or proficient scores on standardized assessments, more than half of the teachers in three of the five districts thought the mathematics curriculum was too difficult for students scoring below basic levels (about 40 percent of

Figure 2.1
Percentage of Mathematics and Language Arts Teachers Reporting That the Curriculum Was Too Difficult for the Lowest-Performing Students in 2014

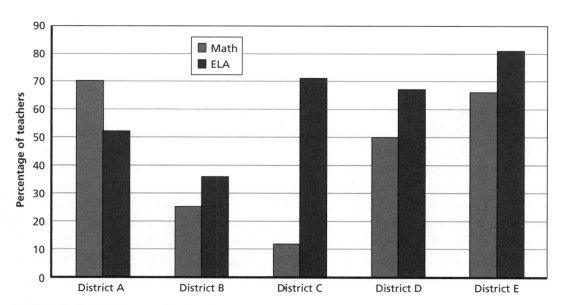

SOURCE: RAND 2014 Summer Teacher Survey.
NOTES: Teachers were asked to "indicate how well the [math or ELA] curriculum matched the ability levels of students in your class." Teachers selected responses among the following options: "The [math or ELA] curriculum was (1) too difficult, (2) just right, or (3) too easy for (a) the students far below grade level in [math or ELA] (Level 1), (b) students somewhat below grade level in [math or ELA] (Level 2), (c) students at grade level in [math or ELA] (Level 3), and (d) students above grade level in math [math or ELA] (Level 4)."
RAND *RR1557-2.1*

Figure 2.2
Percentage of Mathematics and Language Arts Teachers Reporting That the Curriculum Was Too Easy for the Highest-Performing Students in 2014

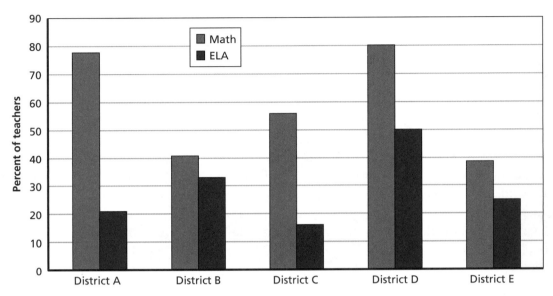

SOURCE: RAND 2014 Summer Teacher Survey.
NOTES: Teachers were asked to "indicate how well the math (ELA) curriculum matched the ability levels of students in your class." Teachers selected responses among the following options: "The [math or ELA] curriculum was (1) too difficult, (2) just right, or (3) too easy for (a) the students far below grade level in [math or ELA] (Level 1), (b) students somewhat below grade level in [math or ELA] (Level 2), (c) students at grade level in [math or ELA] (Level 3), and (d) students above grade level in [math or ELA] (Level 4)."
RAND RR1557-2.2

treatment students). Likewise, in four out of five districts, more than half of language arts teachers thought the same about their curriculum. At the other end of the performance spectrum, more than half of the teachers in three of the five districts thought the mathematics curriculum was too easy for students scoring at the advanced level (about 14 percent of treatment students). However, very few teachers thought the language arts curriculum was too easy for even the most-advanced students. In Chapter Five, we explore whether teachers' opinions of curricular alignment are related to students' outcomes.

Some researchers and practitioners support differentiation as a method for varying instruction within a classroom so that it is targeted differently to students based on skill levels. Recent research supports this practice for reading interventions, finding promise in creating small groups of students with similar knowledge and skills and targeting instruction accordingly (Connor and Morrison, 2016). In both 2013 and 2014, the summer program leaders attempted to differentiate using distinctive approaches. In some cases, small groups were created within classrooms. In others, students were grouped together based on ability in one subject (e.g., mathematics), and these students rotated to other subject classes as a cohort. However, teachers reported in interviews and on our surveys that they did not have data on students before the program began to group them properly. Even when the students had been grouped for them, the materials they had did not allow them to efficiently develop tasks for multiple groups of students, launch lessons for each group, and monitor each student's learning.

Based on RAND classroom observations, independent practice was the most common time when teachers could individualize instruction, either by giving additional activities to students who easily completed tasks or by spending extra time reviewing concepts with struggling students. We rarely observed teachers augmenting the curriculum with additional worksheets or content, and thus the advanced students did not appear to be as challenged as they could have been during the independent work time we observed. Instead, the teachers we observed typically spent all or most of a 15–30 minute independent practice session with the few students who were struggling the most (or were misbehaving) and did not circulate to check in with each student.[2]

Instructional Quality

We rated the quality of instruction in a sample of observed classrooms using a rubric included in online Appendix B. In summer 2013, we observed 282 language arts and 178 mathematics classes; in 2014, we observed 163 language arts and 147 mathematics classes. From the rubric, we created an instructional quality scale derived from eight items (further described in online Appendix D):

1. A large majority of students are on-task throughout class period (scored 1 if yes).
2. Teacher: (1) performs ongoing assessment throughout the whole class period by checking for students' understanding of content and (2) addresses misunderstanding if and as they arise (scored 1 if yes).
3. Explanation of the instructional content was unclear, hard to follow, incomplete, or inconsistent (scored 1 if no).
4. Teacher provided or failed to correct factually inaccurate information that would confuse students about the content and skills they were to learn (scored 1 if no).
5. When the teacher disciplined students, the majority of the class was interrupted for a long period (scored 1 if no).
6. Teacher responsible for the activity was disengaged in the classroom because of distractions by factors that were within her control (scored 1 if no).
7. All or almost all students exhibited obvious signs of enthusiasm for the class throughout the class period (e.g., jumping out of seat, quickly and enthusiastically answering teacher's questions) (scored 1 if yes).

---

[2] It is important to note that our observations, while numerous, represent only about 10 percent of total academic instruction in each of language arts and mathematics.

8.   Prior to students doing independent practice, teacher states the purpose for what they will do (i.e., why students would learn the skill in terms of real world relevance) (scored 1 if yes).

Our measure focused on clear and purposeful instruction, with on-task teachers and students, and with teachers ensuring that each student understood the material during the observed lesson.[3] At best, a classroom could score an 8 on this scale and at worst 0.

Not surprisingly, based on our observations of sampled classrooms, we found that quality varied by classroom—just as other research has found to be the case during the school year, even within the same school building (e.g., Baird et al., 2016). The average mathematics class scored 5.9 in summer 2013, and the average language arts class scored 5.7. The average mathematics class scored 6.2 in summer 2014, and the average language arts class scored 5.8. In both summers, on items 1, 3, 4, 5, and 6 above, we tended to record favorable instructional practices. However, teachers assessed all students' learning and addressed each occurrence of misunderstanding (item 2) in just under half of our observations. We did not observe many classes full of enthusiastic students (item 7), and we rarely observed the purpose of a lesson explained in terms of real-world relevance (item 8).

Overall, the quality of instruction we observed improved slightly from summer 2013 to summer 2014. For instance, in the 2014 sample of classrooms, a higher percentage of teachers (46 percent) checked each student's understanding of content during the lesson we observed and worked with each student who had a misunderstanding than occurred in 2013 (39 percent). Although this proportion increased in 2014, it still represents fewer than half of the classrooms we observed. In Chapter Five, we explore whether students' outcomes are related to instructional quality scores. We deemed students as having "high" quality instruction if their classroom scores on our index were at least one standard deviation above the mean.

Academic Time on Task

Prior research, including our own, has demonstrated the importance of the time dedicated to academic instruction (Harnischfeger and Wiley, 1976; Lomax and Cooley, 1979; Fisher et al., 1980; Karweit and Slavin, 1982; Hawley et al., 1984; Karweit, 1985; McCombs et al., 2014). It is important that students attend summer programs to benefit from them, but it is equally important that, when they are in attendance, they are focused on learning.

---

[3] There are other measures of quality that we could have used and that are used in other instructional quality observation rubrics. For example, we were unable to capture aspects of rigor, including the depth or frequency of teachers' questions or the depth or duration of students' discussions. We attempted to evaluate other aspects of quality, such as these, but failed to reach inter-rater agreement among our team of multiple observers.

In both 2013 and 2014, we estimated the time students spent on language arts and mathematics in the five programs. To conduct these estimations, we considered four sources of data:

1. the master schedule from the districts, with the number of minutes of mathematics and language arts instruction to be provided each day, and the number of program days
2. the average start and end times of mathematics and language arts classes for each site, based on our daily observations of classes
3. the number of minutes actually dedicated to academic instruction within these class periods, based again on our sample of instruction (Here, for example, we deducted minutes for bathroom and snack breaks or for nonacademic tasks such as unplanned coloring breaks during the academic classes.)
4. the average number of days a typical student attended in each district.

To derive information for the second and third items, we kept a time log during our classroom observations, recording the minutes when the majority of students were in the room and when the teacher launched and ended the class and minute-by-minute notes on class segments to track instructional and noninstructional time during the enacted class period. For example, we noted such things as a class that was scheduled to begin at 10:00 a.m. but actually launched at 10:11 a.m.; a class that lost a combined total of six minutes to noninstructional activities, such as a bathroom break; and a class that ended at 10:59 a.m. when it was scheduled to end at 11:00 a.m.

With these classroom observation data linked to student classroom rosters, we created student-level indicators of academic time on task for mathematics and language arts that equal the product of the following three measures: (1) the number of days a given student attended the summer program, multiplied by (2) the average number of hours that observed mathematics/language arts classes lasted (meaning the enacted time from class launch to class wrap-up, regardless of scheduled class time), averaged across the subject-relevant classes we observed within a given site, multiplied by (3) the average percentage of enacted class time that was devoted to instruction.

As noted above, our observations of classrooms only account for about 10 percent of all instruction in each subject (language arts and mathematics). In an attempt to correct for outlier classrooms (e.g., a substitute teacher might have spent less time on instruction because of time lost to building new relationships), we first averaged observed time to the classroom (when classrooms were observed more than once), then to teachers (when teachers were observed teaching the same subject more than once but to different groups of students), and then to the site. We have confidence in the attendance data, and average student attendance is an important component of the academic time-on-task estimate. Nonetheless, the resulting numbers represent estimates of received minutes of instruction rather than exact calculations.

Figures 2.3 and 2.4 present the estimated academic time on task that students received for language arts and for mathematics by district in 2014. Data from 2013 are very similar. In both summers, fewer hours of academic instruction were provided than intended. When we estimated minutes of instruction provided, the proportion of hours of instruction provided ranged from 78 percent to 90 percent of the intended hours. This percentage is similar to what others have found in observations of academic time on task during the school year (e.g., Smith, 1998), indicating that some loss of instructional time may be inevitable. In one district, the plan was to provide 38 hours of language arts instruction over the summer, out of a 150-hour program. After deducting noninstructional minutes based on our classroom observations in the summer sites in that district (which is a small sample of all instruction over the summer), a student with perfect attendance would have received about 31 hours of language arts instruction. But not all students had perfect attendance, as we will discuss in more detail in Chapter Four. In that same district, students attended an average of 60 percent of the summer program days. So, the average attender in this district received about 19 hours

Figure 2.3
Discrepancy Between Intended and Average Instructional Hours Received in Mathematics by District, 2014

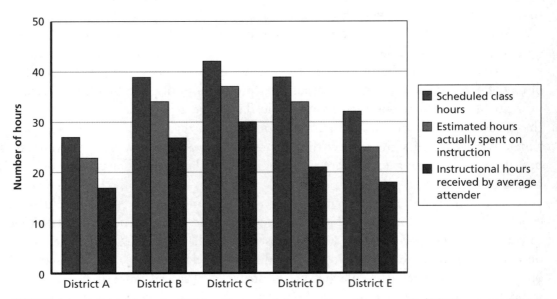

SOURCE: School districts' summer 2014 written schedules, summer attendance, and RAND summer 2014 classroom observations.
NOTES: Scheduled class hours based on 2014 written schedules, estimated hours actually spent on instruction based on RAND classroom observations, instructional hours received by average attender calculated considering actual hours of instruction and average student attendance.
RAND *RR1557-2.3*

Figure 2.4
Discrepancy Between Intended and Average Instructional Hours Received in Language Arts by District, 2014

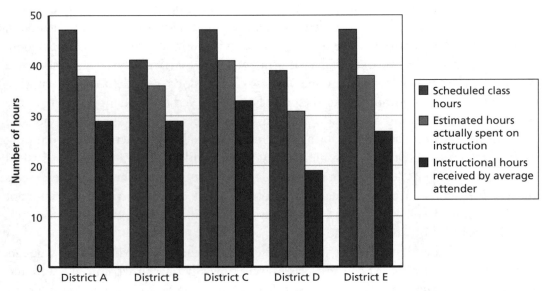

SOURCE: School districts' summer 2014 written schedules, summer attendance, and RAND summer 2014 classroom observations.
NOTES: Scheduled class hours based on 2014 written schedules, estimated hours actually spent on instruction based on RAND classroom observations, instructional hours received by average attender calculated considering actual hours of instruction and average student attendance.
RAND RR1557-2.4

of language arts instruction instead of the planned 38 hours. In the district with the highest ADA rates, our estimates suggest that an average student received 29 hours of language arts instruction instead of the 40 hours that were planned.

In Chapter Five, we examine the link between students' academic time on task and their outcomes.

Enrichment Opportunities

In each year of the study, students participated in enrichment activities in all of the district summer programs. These activities were opportunities that students might not otherwise have had during the summer, such as sailing, theater, visual arts, swimming, and rock climbing. In addition to helping close the opportunity gap, enrichment classes were intended to make the programs fun and engaging for students so that they would attend consistently. Based on our enrichment observations—which totaled 240 in summer 2013 and 207 in summer 2014 and ranged from 15 to 76 per district depending on the number of students served in the program—students remained on task during these enrichment periods, working together in classes with a small number of other students. However, student enthusiasm for enrichment activities varied across districts: In one district, students showed enthusiasm in 36 percent of our enrichment observations; in another, it was 65 percent. We do not examine links between enrichment quality or student enthusiasm and students outcomes, but we do describe examples of observed variation by classroom, which appeared to be based on the nature of the activity and the quality of the instruction.

As an example, we observed that students were particularly enthusiastic in a swimming class in one district. In one of these class periods, a student was attempting to address her fear of jumping into the pool. Peers observed the student standing at the edge of the pool making motions to jump in. These peers climbed out of the pool and stood next to her on the edge, offering to jump in while holding her hand or jumping in first to demonstrate that it was safe. They said things like, "You can do it," and asked how they could help her. When the student finally jumped into the pool, these peers and the lifeguards cheered. In each of our observations of this particular enrichment activity, the students were enthusiastic. They received individual instruction for their specific level of skill, and they had fun.

At the other end of the spectrum, we observed enrichment activities where students were distinctly unenthusiastic. These classes were typically ones in which there were too few activities for the time allotted or tasks that did not engage or challenge the students. For example, we saw some enrichment periods spanning 120 minutes of coloring and "free drawing." We also observed teachers bringing store-bought puzzles into class for the students to work on during the entire enrichment period. Bored students often acted out and caused supervisory challenges. Most enrichment instructors were community based, rather than district teachers, and we learned through our interviews that enrichment instructors often had less experience in both instruction and behavior management.

Site Climate

The climate of a school, defined in general as the quality and nature of school life, has been associated with various positive student outcomes, including student attendance. One researcher has calculated that as many as 160,000 students nationwide may stay home from school on any given day because they are afraid of being bullied (Nansel et al., 2001). Others have found, more generally, that positive school climates are correlated with decreased student absenteeism (Purkey and Smith, 1983; Reid, 1983; Sommer, 1985; deJung and Duckworth, 1986; Rumberger, 1987; Gottfredson and Gottfredson, 1989).

We created three measures of climate. Across these three measures, we mainly observed positive climates, but there were exceptions. In Chapter Five, we explore whether scores on these measures are related to student outcomes.

Our first measure was based on our classroom observations, and we refer to it as positive instructional climate. As with instructional quality, we created an index to measure it. This index was based on the following seven indicators of instructional climate:

1. Students verbally encourage each other and are overtly friendly and supportive (scored 1 if yes).
2. Teacher shows explicit signs of caring and positive affect toward youth (scored 1 if yes).
3. Students show explicit signs that they have warm, positive affect to teacher (scored 1 if yes).
4. The teacher explicitly taught social skills such as respecting, listening, cooperating with, or helping others or teaching of politeness (scored 1 if yes).
5. In at least one instance, the teacher was disrespectful to students (scored 1 if no).
6. There was one or more flagrant instance of student misbehavior (scored 1 if no).
7. The teacher responsible for the activity was disengaged in the classroom because of distractions by factors that were within her control (scored 1 if no).

Using this index, we created a score by site, averaging the scores for the classrooms within that site. At best, a classroom could score 7 on this scale, and at worst 0.

In 2014, the average positive instructional climate scale score ranged from a low of 3.9 in one site to a high of 6.0 in another. The average index score was 4.4, which was a very slight increase from 2013, when the average index score was 4.3 and ranged from a low of 3.3 in one site to a high of 6.2 in another. But there were notable differences across districts and across sites within a district. For example, in one site we observed in 2013, only 44 percent of the teachers we observed in classroom observations were respectful to students. We observed negative behavior, including yelling, as well as what our observers judged to be rude, dismissive, and sarcastic language. In another site that same year, the teachers demonstrated consistent respect toward students in 100 percent of the classrooms we observed.

Our second measure of climate is based on our teacher survey, and we refer to it as "site discipline and order." Teachers reported very positive site climates in both 2013 and 2014. We report data from 2014 here. In that year, the vast majority of surveyed teachers (from 85 percent to 100 percent) reported that the program was well managed, that they liked teaching in the summer program (from 92 percent to 100 percent), and that they believed students enjoyed the program (from 83 percent to 100 percent). In four of the five districts, few teachers (0 percent to 15 percent) reported that students got into physical fights on a weekly basis. Similarly, few teachers (0 percent to 19 percent) reported that students bullied, harassed, or teased one another in four of the five districts. In the fifth district, however, the responses were more troubling: 33 percent of teachers reported physical fighting, and 42 percent of teachers reported student bullying, harassing, or teasing on a weekly basis. This district also struggled to ensure consistent student attendance. In Chapter Five, we examine whether a measure of "site discipline and order," which is based on teacher reports of bullying and fighting, is related to student outcomes.

Our third measure of climate is based on observations of the entire site, and we refer to it as "daily site climate." Almost every time observers visited a site to observe classrooms, they recorded aspects of site climate, with a particular focus on staff-to-student and student-to-student interactions (see online Appendix B for details on this process and the observation rubric). In total, we conducted 154 of these site climate observations in summer 2014. (This was a new measure in 2014; we did not collect these data in summer 2013.) Our observations were spread across the 34 total summer sites within the five school districts.

With the exception of one district, in which our observers marked "neutral" on average, our observers tended to agree that staff members were overtly friendly and warm toward students. We noted student enjoyment of their time with staff and some poignant moments of playfulness. We typically observed instructors and students interacting as friends; on many occasions, students ran up to teachers and hugged them. There were a few observations of negative staff-to-student interactions, however, such as disparaging comments about students as they engaged in enrichment activities or yelling at students during lunch, recess, and enrichment.

We were less likely to observe students being overtly friendly and supportive toward one another, with observers marking this item "neutral," on average, in three of the five districts. Unfortunately, we observed physical fighting and student bullying, name-calling, and screaming. In some cases, the nearby adults ignored this behavior. However, we did witness students laughing together during classroom tasks that they enjoyed. We also observed students cheering other students on when they were performing (e.g., in a play) or when they were swimming (as previously described) or rock climbing.

Program Revenue and Costs

The cost of an intervention is a primary consideration for districts weighing options for raising student achievement. Using methods we describe in online Appendix B, we gathered cost and revenue data from the five participating school districts for the planning and execution of the summer 2014 program. (We did not collect cost data for the summer 2013 programs.) In an attempt to provide information relevant for other school districts, we calculated the costs of the studied summer learning programs that served multiple grade levels. While the focus of the randomized controlled trial was on the cohort of rising fifth-graders in 2014, three of the districts offered the summer program to multiple grade levels, ranging from kindergarten through eighth grade.

The costs presented here are for those entire programs—as opposed to only the costs associated with the study cohort.[4]

Note that the summer programs have been in operation since at least 2010. As a result, they are relatively mature, and the cost estimates presented here reflect the cost of offering an ongoing summer program rather than launching a new program. In addition, we focus on the "new money" needed to sustain a district-led summer program and exclude in-kind contributions, primarily in the form of staff time and the use of existing facilities, because we were unable to determine the reliability of districts' reporting of in-kind support. We do highlight, however, examples of in-kind contributions to show how they can support summer programs. These estimates are intended to help decisionmakers understand the costs of offering an ongoing district-led summer program for multiple grade levels. In addition to these annual recurring costs, districts that are just starting a summer program should anticipate start-up costs for activities such as identifying a new curriculum (as opposed to buying replacement materials), forming partnerships with enrichment providers, or identifying new vendors (e.g., for transportation).

Revenue

We examined revenue sources for all five districts, which revealed a wide variety of funding portfolios to support the summer programs. Sources included private foundations, general funds from district budgets, Title I funding, and federal meal reimbursements. Across the districts, there were variations in the funding mix. Two of the five districts used little or no general district funds but did use Title I funding, while the remaining three districts used general funds but not Title I. All five districts used federal meal reimbursements and, to varying extents, funding from private foundations. The sources of revenue to support these programs have shifted over time, based on available funding. In 2011, these programs relied heavily on Title I funding following an influx through the American Recovery and Reinvestment Act (Augustine et al., 2013). From 2011 to 2014, there was a significant reduction in Title I funding, which was made up through an increase in private foundation and general district funds.

Per-Student Costs

Across the three districts offering programs at multiple grade levels, the cost per attending student (i.e., attending at least one day of the program) for the 2014 summer programs ranged from $1,070 to $1,700 with an average of $1,340 (Table 2.4). But not all students attended every day. The ADA rate was 77 percent in the three districts, which substantially increases the cost per filled seat. The cost per filled seat—that is, total

---

[4]   We have elected to present cost data without identifying the individual districts in the interest of focusing our discussion on specific cost drivers.

Table 2.4
Per-Student Costs of 2014 Summer Programs Based on Three Programs Serving Multiple Grade Levels

Cost	Average	Low	High
Per student	$1,340.00	$1,070.00	$1,700.00
Per filled seat	$1,860.00	$1,320.00	$2,100.00
Per student per hour	$6.60	$5.70	$7.50
Per filled seat per hour	$9.20	$7.00	$12.40

SOURCE: Summer 2014 planning and execution cost data collected from five study districts.
NOTE: Cost per student is the cost per students who attended for at least one day. The cost per filled seat is the cost per students present, on average, each day.

cost divided by the average number of students present per day—ranged from $1,320 to $2,675, with an average of $1,860. These translate to an average hourly cost of $6.70 per student and $9.20 per filled seat. As a point of reference, school-year costs in these districts ranged from $7.65 to $20.06 per hour, and the 2013 national average school-year costs were $10.52 per student per hour (Cornman, 2015).

These summer program cost estimates align with those from prior studies. Yeh (2010) estimated summer program costs of $1,515 per attending student. In 2011, we found that the average costs from six district programs were $7 to $13 per student per hour and $8 to $19 per filled seat per hour (Augustine et al., 2013).

Expenses

Figure 2.5 shows the average expenditures for the 2014 summer learning programs in the three districts serving multiple grade levels. Note that the three largest cost categories—academics, enrichment, and district and site management—account for roughly 85 percent of total costs. Personnel is by far the largest driver of the overall costs of a program, making up the majority of total expenses:

- Academic classroom staff salaries account for 35 percent of total expenditures, with district teacher salaries accounting for the vast majority of the costs in this category. Salaries for paraprofessionals, substitute teachers, and interns are also included but make up only 4 percent of this category.
- District and site administration, which accounts for 25 percent of total expenditures, includes central-office administrative positions as well as site-based program leaders and nonteaching staff, such as guidance counselors and school administrative assistants.
- Enrichment is the third largest source of costs. This includes field trips and district-employed music and physical education teachers, but the majority (85 percent) of enrichment costs was for contracted services with community-based organizations.

Figure 2.5
2014 Average Summer Learning Program Expenditures in Three Districts

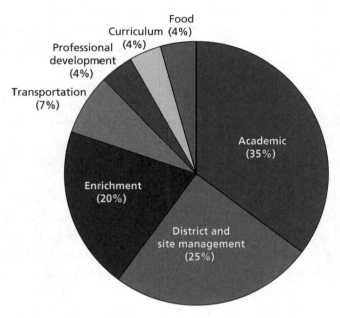

SOURCE: RAND estimates from summer 2014 cost data.
NOTE: Numbers do not add to 100 percent due to rounding.
RAND RR1557-2.5

- Transportation, which accounts for 7 percent of total average expenditures, is primarily for daily busing but also includes transportation to and from field trips.
- The curriculum category (4 percent) includes both district-level curricular personnel (who helped select the curriculum and write pacing guides) and the ongoing costs to replace or update curriculum materials used in the classrooms.
- Professional development costs (4 percent) are primarily driven by the cost of teachers' time for two to three days of professional development.
- Food accounts for an estimated 4 percent of total expenses, much of which was reimbursed through the federal meals program.

Across the three districts, there were some variations in the breakdown of expenses. Academic salaries ranged from 23 percent to 50 percent, because of differences in teacher costs or the number of hours that teachers worked during the day. One program had full-day schedules for district-employed teachers, while others offered a half-day academic teaching load with a half-day of enrichment provided by community-based organizations. In addition, hourly rates for district-employed academic teachers ranged from a flat $20 per hour for one program to $27–$56 per hour in another program, depending on the teacher's salary step.

While enrichment costs were fairly consistent across the three programs, district and site administrative costs ranged from 16 percent to 32 percent of overall costs. This variation was largely driven by differences in the number of central-office administrative staff dedicated to summer programming and differences in the number of summer site–based, nonteacher positions, such as site leaders, site coordinators, administrative staff, counselors, and behavior coordinators. Transportation costs ranged from 3 percent to 13 percent.

In-Kind Costs

Although all districts provided in-kind support for the summer programs in various forms, it is difficult to estimate the full scope and value of those contributions. However, estimates provided by two districts provide some insight into school- and district-level in-kind contributions.

One district provided an estimate of the time spent by central office administrative staff during the summer months. These are full-time district employees who dedicate some time to supporting the summer program but are not paid out of the summer budget. For a summer program of roughly 2,000 students, in-kind contributions during the 25-day summer program were as follows: the director of operations (25 percent time) who managed the staff overseeing the summer program; an information technology coordinator (5 percent time); a food service coordinator (25 percent time); and a curriculum supervisor (10 percent time during the summer program). This district also provided some year-round support from the finance and legal departments. Using broad assumptions about salaries, the above in-kind contributions equate to roughly 3 percent of the total program cost.

A second example of in-kind contributions was from a district that used assistant principals to serve as site leaders for the summer programs. Assistant principals were full-time, year-round employees who were paid for out of the district's general funds. Using them as site leaders for the summer program reduced the amount of "new money" needed to run the program by approximately 5 percent.[5]

While these contributions can reduce the financial burden of running a summer program, it is important to recognize that there is an opportunity cost associated with staff time. Asking existing employees to take on additional responsibilities may come at the expense of other activities.

---

[5] Note that we generally excluded in-kind contributions from the costs presented in this chapter. However, because we considered site leaders to be such a core part of a summer program, we did include the relevant portion of the assistant principals' salaries in our cost totals.

Conclusions on Implementation

In this chapter, we described how the summer programs were enacted. Program leaders effectively implemented the common research-based features required for study inclusion. Beyond those requirements, they had autonomy over other aspects of their programs. For example, the study specified the employment of certified teachers, but program leaders had discretion over specific hiring practices.

Leaders did face challenges in implementation. Not all districts hired teachers with relevant grade-level or subject-matter expertise. Most teachers found the curriculum to be too challenging for their most struggling students. Differentiation proved challenging given that teachers were provided with one set of curricular activities. In only about half of our observations did we note that teachers checked in with each student and then worked to ensure that those who were struggling mastered the content.

We did tend to see clear instruction and on-task teachers and students in the classrooms. However, many students received far less instruction than program leaders had planned and hoped for.

Students did appear to enjoy the enrichment opportunities, although our observations noted variation in student enthusiasm during these activities.

Teachers' impressions of students' experiences were quite favorable, with the vast majority reporting that students enjoyed the programs. Teachers in turn enjoyed teaching in them and reported that the programs were well managed. This belief corresponds to our observations: We noted that operational logistics—such as busing, food services, and transportation—ran more smoothly each summer, dating back to our 2011 observations. We also observed that throughout the day, most adults had warm, positive interactions with the students.

Finally, we determined that, across the three districts offering programs at multiple grade levels, the cost per attending student (i.e., attending at least one day of the program) for the 2014 summer programs ranged from $1,070 to $1,700, with an average of $1,340. Subsequent chapters present information on students' outcomes, to provide additional insights into the cost-effectiveness of the programs. But first, we turn to students' attendance rates to expand on our understanding of the amount of academic time on task students received each summer.

CHAPTER THREE

Attendance: A Critical Element of Summer Programming

When designing the study, we started from the common-sense premise that attendance at a summer program is required to reap positive effects. Because of its importance, we collected detailed data on summer program attendance and the steps that districts took to encourage students to attend. We describe attendance rates and patterns in this chapter. In Chapter Five, we analyze the differences in student outcomes for those with high attendance compared with those with lower attendance.

Overview

As described in Chapter One, in April 2013, families of 5,637 students submitted applications for the opportunity to attend two consecutive summers of free programming. Of these applicants, 3,192 students were admitted.[1] Since attendance in the five- to six-week summer programs was voluntary, we expected that not all students who had applied would attend, and that those who attended the programs would do so at rates lower than during the mandatory school year. We expected lower rates of attendance because, unlike the school year, there are no penalties for absence. Furthermore, one might expect higher no-show rates in the second summer compared with the first because 14 months elapsed between when families first signed up for access to two consecutive summers of free programming and the first day of the summer 2014 program. As we describe below, these expectations bore out.

To put summer program attendance in context, we present four attendance categories for the 3,192 treatment group students who were offered a seat in two consecutive years of summer programs (Figure 3.1). We categorize the students by whether they

---

[1] This number excludes two students whose parents withdrew consent for their children to participate in the study.

- did not attend a single day of the summer program because they moved out of the district or shifted to a school outside of the district[2]
- did not attend a single day of the summer program for other reasons
- attended between one and 19 days of a given summer session,[3] which we define as low attendance[4]
- attended 20 or more days of the summer session, which we define as high attendance.

As Figure 3.1 illustrates, there are differences in attendance patterns in the two summers. The most striking difference is that many more students did not participate in the second summer: 11 percent of students had moved out of the district by then, and another 37 percent did not attend for other reasons. Taken together, nearly half the treatment students (48 percent) did not attend for a single day of the 2014 summer program; put another way, of all the students who attended in summer 2013, 57 percent attended for at least one day in summer 2014. It must be remembered, however, that the no-show rate in summer 2014 is a special case: It is the return rate among students who signed up and were accepted to attend both the summer 2013 and 2014 programs about 14 months earlier. The 14-month time lag between the original commitment and first day of the summer 2014 program increased the possibility that families' plans changed by the second summer or that their preferences shifted, compared with the first summer, when there was only a two-month lag between enrolling and the program starting. Partly because of this attrition from one summer to the next, both the low attenders and the high attenders in 2014 were a smaller proportion of the treatment group in the second summer. As we describe in Chapter Four, that fact reduced the ability to detect effects of summer programming on the entire, original treatment group.

Having detailed attendance data allowed us to trace the flow of students from one level of attendance to another between the two summer programs, as shown in Figure 3.2. For example, we found that many low-attending students in summer 2013 either moved out of the district (11 percent) or did not show up in the second summer for other reasons (49 percent). Another 14 percent converted to high attenders in summer 2014. The rest (25 percent) remained low attenders in the second summer.

---

[2]   If a student attended no days at a public school in the original school district in the subsequent school year, we assume conservatively that the student had moved away by the time the summer program had started in June. However, it is possible that some students had not yet moved by June or remained in place but enrolled in either a private school or in a charter school not belonging to the school district.

[3]   Based on an analysis that we describe in online Appendix D, we found that treatment effects were greatest for students attending at least 15 to 25 days, where the minimum days varied depending on which year and set of students we examined. To define a consistent threshold, we defined high attendance as 20 or more days, and low attendance as 1–19 days in a given summer.

[4]   We recognize that attending 19 days, or close to that amount, might not be considered "low" attendance by all, but use this term simply to refer to a group of students that are neither no-shows nor "high" attenders per the study's definition.

Figure 3.1
Breakdown of Treatment Students' Attendance in Summers 2013 and 2014

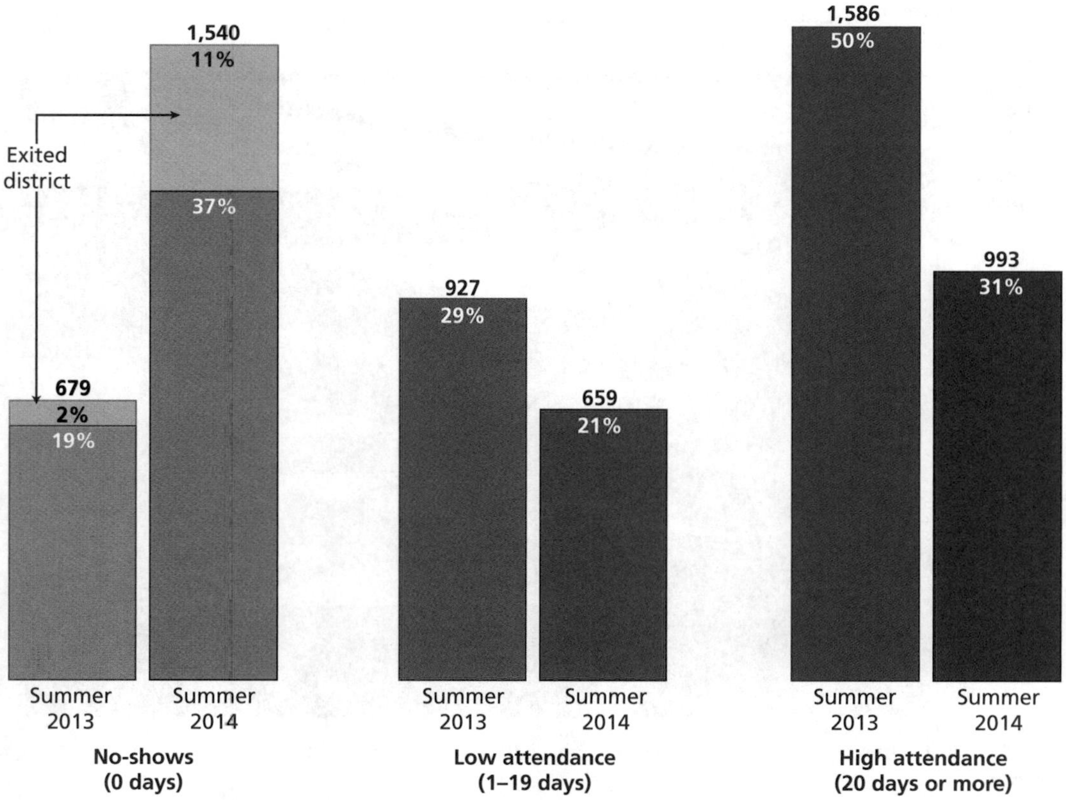

SOURCE: RAND analysis of districts' summer 2013 and 2014 attendance data.
NOTES: The numbers at the top of the bars are numbers of students in that category; percentages reflect proportion of the treatment group in that category.
RAND RR1557-3.1

It might be expected that students who were loosely connected to the program in 2013 could disconnect entirely as of summer 2014. It is more surprising to see that a substantial portion of high attenders in summer 2013 reduced their involvement in the second summer: One-fifth became no-shows, and one-fifth slipped to low attenders in the second summer so that the group of high attenders in 2014 was about one-third smaller than it was the year before. Nonetheless, the majority of high attenders in 2014 were also high attenders in summer 2013.

District Attempts to Reduce No-Show Rates

The school districts knew that a substantial portion of students might be no-shows in summer 2013 based on the two prior years of summer programming. In response, they

Figure 3.2
Fluctuation in Attendance Among Treatment Students from the First to Second Summer

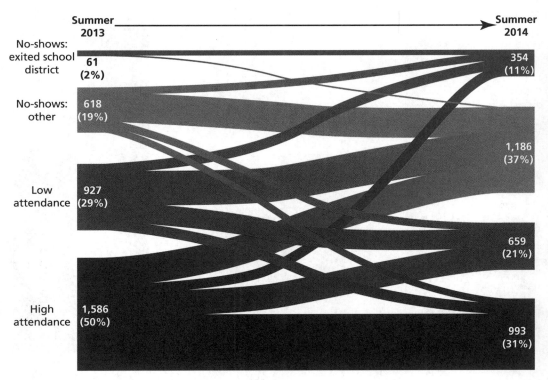

SOURCE: RAND analysis of districts' summer 2013 and 2014 attendance data.
RAND RR1557-3.2

engaged in a number of strategies to reduce that number in 2013 and again in 2014. We catalogue those activities in Table 3.1 based on meeting minutes and documents provided by a third-party marketing firm that aided the districts in these efforts. With its help, each district created and implemented recruitment plans. For example, in the months that elapsed between the April 2013 lottery and the start dates of the 2013 summer program, the school districts hosted a series of activities ranging from holding open houses for parents, sending home fliers in backpacks, and placing reminder phone calls to parents. One district even had teachers write individualized letters to their students to encourage them to attend.

Districts continued and even increased their efforts for summer 2014 by reminding students throughout the 2013–2014 school year that they should return for summer 2014. For example, many districts sent admitted students promotional materials such as water bottles, fanny packs, or pens with the logo of the summer program and also held events during the year at which student "alumni" of the summer programs talked about the fun they had in prior years. The level of effort varied by district. As an example of high effort, one district during the 2013–2014 school year hired 34 "engagement coordina-

Table 3.1
Activities to Reduce No-Shows in Summer 2013 and 2014

Activities	District				
	A	B	C	D	E
Establishing a deadline for enrollment in summer program	2013 2014	2013 2014	2013 2014	2013 2014	2013 2014
Instituting an attendance policy and communicating it to parents		2013 2014	2013 2014		2013 2014
Writing personalized letters to admitted students	2013 2014				
Writing reminders (e.g., emails, fliers sent home in backpacks)	2013 2014	2013 2014	2013 2014	2013 2014	2013 2014
Placing robocalls to parents	2013 2014	2013 2014	2013 2014		
Placing personalized calls to parents	2013 2014		2013* 2014*		2014
Giving students promotional material (e.g., backpacks, mugs, key rings) to encourage them to come to the summer program	2013 2014		2014		2013 2014
Presenting information in school for admitted students (e.g., slide show, student testimonial)					2013 2014
Holding parent events (e.g., open house for admitted students, baseball game)	2013 2014		2013 2014		2013 2014
Making home visits to parents of admitted students				2014	
Having school-based staff serve as "engagement coordinators" in each sending school					2014

* Some, not all, of district schools.

tors." These were teachers (one teacher per school in each of the 34 schools where the summer students attended) who organized, executed, and submitted monthly logs about their student engagement activities for a $3,000 stipend. At a minimum, each engagement coordinator during the 2013–2014 school year was asked to do several things: Send four mailings home per child, meet in person or call each child's parents three times, collect from each parent a signed renewal form, hold at least one in-school student "reunion" for the summer school enrollees, and help organize one family event that pooled students from all sending schools to the given summer site. As an example of lower effort, another district placed robocalls and sent home fliers in student backpacks.

The evidence suggests that, unlike daily attendance, which we discuss below, districts' efforts were modestly successful in reducing no-shows. Districts increased their efforts from summer 2012, prior to the current experiment, to summer 2013, and Figure 3.3 shows that no-show rates did decline in the two districts for which we have data. Further, the districts that expended the most effort on recruitment and reengagement as of spring 2013 saw the greatest declines in the no-show rates from summer 2012 to summer 2013. For example, one district's increased recruitment efforts in spring 2013 corresponded with a no-show rate that declined from 24 percent in summer 2012 to 17 percent in summer 2013. In another district, where the district set a firm enrollment cut-off date in spring 2013 and frequently reminded parents of the program, the no-show rate of 45 percent in summer 2012 shrank to 27 percent in summer 2013. In a third district, where teachers wrote a personalized letter to students, only 8 percent of students never attended.

Figure 3.3 also shows that the rate of no-shows increased substantially in 2014. Looking at the total column, a little under half (48 percent) of the 3,192 admitted students were no-shows in the second summer. That includes 11 percent of students who moved out of the district, leaving 37 percent as "voluntary" no-shows who theoretically could have attended since they remained in the district. These second-year no-shows are a special case in the sense that they represent the no-show rate among students who were accepted into the program 14 months before. The second-year no-show rate is important in that it limits the potential impacts that offering two years of summer programming can have on the entire treatment group. Also, the lower return rate in the second year indicates that school districts that operate voluntary summer programs for multiple grade levels might not expect a large majority of their students to return from one year to the next. Beyond that, the summer 2014 no-show rate has limited policy relevance in that school districts are unlikely to replicate the early, two-year admission process that was required for this research study.

Figure 3.3
No-Show Rates Among Treatment Students by District and Overall

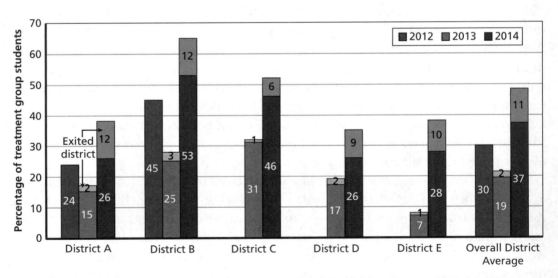

NOTES: No-show rates are not available in summer 2012 for three districts. Summer 2012 data do not distinguish between no-show students who exited the district and the other no-show students who remain in district.

Attendance Patterns and Districts' Attempts to Increase Attendance

Promoting regular attendance is a second and different challenge from persuading admitted students to show up for the summer program. To characterize student attendance, we examined two dimensions. The first is ADA, which is a metric that school districts commonly use and helps to determine the level of staffing needed based on the typical number of students present on a given day. The second is the number of days individual students attended each summer and over the two summers to categorize the "dose" of summer programming they received.

Average Daily Attendance

The ADA is the average proportion of students present on a given day. Another way to understand ADA is as the percentage of total summer program days that the typical attender came.

Four patterns stand out:

1. As anticipated, students attended voluntary summer programs at substantially lower rates than during the mandatory school year. As shown in the "total" column of Figure 3.4, those who attended the summer program at all typically attended for 74 percent of summer program days in summer 2013 (and in summer 2012 and summer 2014). By comparison, these same students attended 96 percent of the days during the 2013–2014 school year. The correlation between students' summer 2013 and 2013–2014 school-year attendance, however, was not particularly high: 0.29.
2. Districts have differential attendance rates. Attendance in three summers was substantially higher in three districts (around 80 percent) than in the other two (60–70 percent).
3. Unlike no-show rates that have fluctuated over the summers, ADA has been relatively stable in each district (see Figure 3.4). With a few exceptions that we note below, districts' efforts to boost daily attendance have not noticeably changed rates.
4. Attendance declined over the course of a summer program. Figure 3.5 shows similar downward slopes in each district's summer 2013 attendance data. (Results for summer 2014 are similar, but not shown.) Attendance regularly dipped on Fridays and on days after holidays such as the Fourth of July.

Number of Days Students Attended Summer Programs

Since the length of the summer programs in the five districts varied, a single attendance rate of 74 percent does not translate into the same number of days attended in each dis-

Figure 3.4
Average Daily Attendance Rate Among Treatment Group Students Who Ever Attended, Summer 2012 to 2014

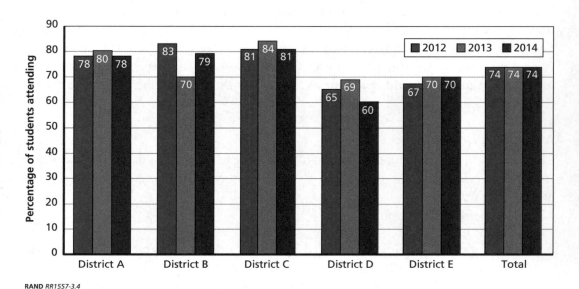

RAND RR1557-3.4

trict.[5] Counting the number of days a student attended the summer program allows us to understand more precisely who got a large or small amount (or dose) of summer programming. We define *high attenders* as those who attended 20 or more days in a given

Figure 3.5
Time Trends in Summer Program Attendance, Summer 2013

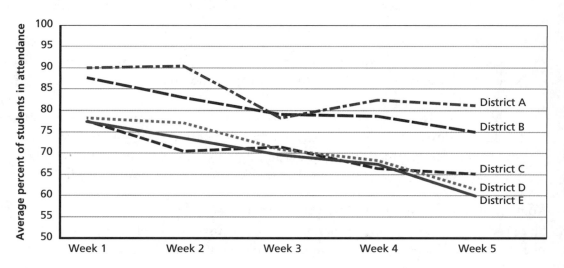

RAND RR1557-3.5

---

[5]   One district had as few as 23 days and another had as many 30 days.

summer, and *low attenders* as those who attended one to 19 days in a given summer.[6] In other words, high attendance can be thought of as attending at least four weeks out of a five-week summer program. Then, looking across both summers, we define *consecutive high attenders* as those who attended 20 or more days in each of the two summers. We employ these classifications in correlational analyses in Chapter Five to distinguish outcomes for low and high attenders in a single summer and in both summers.

Figure 3.6 shows the number of days students attended the summer programs in the two summers. In the figure, we group the number of days attended into bins that approximate the number of weeks students attended. The figure reveals a U-shaped distribution, since students admitted to the summer program clustered in either the no-show or the high-attender categories. Low attenders were spread relatively evenly across the full span of attending up to one week to attending up to four weeks. This spread shows that low attendance was generally not a matter of students showing up at the start of the program, deciding it was not for them, and then opting out.

Another way to look at attendance patterns is to focus only on those who attended one or more days of the summer program (i.e., to exclude the no-shows shown in Figure 3.6). As Figure 3.7 shows, approximately 60 percent of students who attended one or more days were high attenders; in fact, low and high attendance rates for attending students were very similar in the two summers.

Figure 3.6
Number of Days That Treatment Students Attended in Summers 2013 and 2014

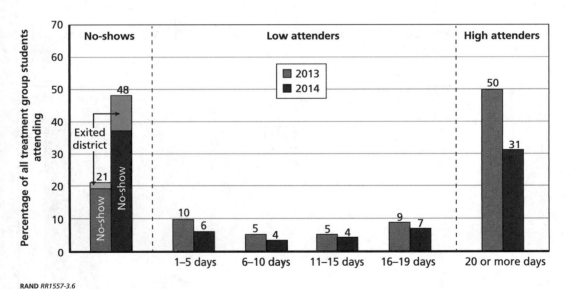

RAND RR1557-3.6

---

[6]   Online Appendix D explains the process we used to determine these definitions.

However, that average disguises distinct district differences. For example, the percentage of high attenders in summer 2013 ranged from a low of 52 percent in one district to a high of 85 percent in another.

We are also interested in the total attendance of students across both summers. Figure 3.8, which considers the proportion of the entire set of 3,192 students offered a spot in the summer programs, shows that 29 percent were consecutive high attenders who attended 20 or more days in each of the two summers. Sixteen percent did not attend a single day of either summer program. (This is lower than the 21 and 48 percent no-show rates in summer 2013 and summer 2014 because some students who attended zero days in summer 2013 attended one or more days in summer 2014 and vice versa.) The balance of the treatment group—55 percent—comprised students who were low attenders in at least one (or both) of the summers.

Characteristics of Attenders

In examining the characteristics of students with different attendance levels, we restrict our discussion to summer 2013 because that is the most comparable to what districts would experience if operating voluntary summer programs outside the confines of a research study. In general, student background characteristics were poor at predicting attendance by treatment group students; however, this was driven mostly by a poor ability to predict no-shows (see Table 3.2). We could not differentiate between no-show students and attending students, based on students' characteristics. We hypothesize

Figure 3.7
Number of Days Attended Among Treatment Group Students Who Attended at Least One Day, Summers 2013 and 2014

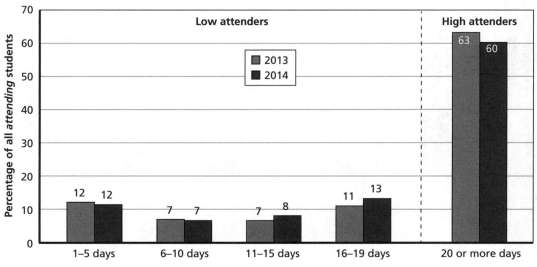

Figure 3.8
Cumulative Days Attended Across Summers 2013 and 2014

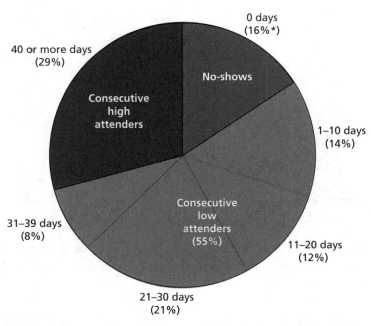

* This is the percentage of students that did not show up for either summer program year.
RAND *RR1557-3.8*

that no-shows may be a mix of students who had low propensity to attend and students who would have attended but were drawn away by an attractive alternative option.

However, comparing just the low- and high-attendance groups to each other, high attenders had statistically significant lower rates of eligibility for free or reduced-price meals, higher attendance rates the prior school year, and lower percentages scoring at the lowest level on prior achievement tests. The race/ethnicity makeup of the two groups also differed, with the high attendance group having more African-Americans and Asians and fewer Hispanics than the low-attendance group. On many of these variables, the no-show group fell somewhere between the low- and high-attendance groups. We controlled for all of the baseline variables shown in Table 3.2 in our statistical models.

Looking at qualitative data, we also note that caring for siblings or relatives during the summer might help explain no-shows and lower attendance: high-attending students were the least likely to report on our fall 2014 survey that they took care of a sibling or relative during summer 2014 (35 percent) compared with no-shows (44 percent), the low-attending group (41 percent), and the control group (40 percent).[7] Alto-

---

[7]   Except for caring for siblings and amount of time spent at summer camps, students reported engaging in similar summer activities regardless of their attendance category. For example, approximately one-third of the control group, no-shows, low attenders, and high attenderes each reported staying mostly in their house during the summer.

Table 3.2
Characteristics of High and Low Attenders in Summer 2013

Student Characteristic	Overall Treatment Group	No-Shows	Low Attenders	High Attenders
Number of students	3,192	679	927	1,586
Percentage of days attended in 2012–2013 school year	95.7	95.0	94.4	96.7
Qualify for free or reduced-price meal	89.1	91.5	93.0	85.8
African-American	49.4	46.7	46.4	52.3
Hispanic	37.8	40.1	42.6	34.1
Asian	2.8	3.7	1.1	3.5
White	7.7	7.2	7.7	7.9
Disability	11.2	8.6	11.0	12.3
Low academic performance on math or ELA spring 2013 test	41.5	33.0	50.7	39.8

gether, we identified five potential reasons for lower attendance based on surveys of summer teachers, surveys of students, and anecdotal observations RAND observers made during site visits:

- a prevailing attitude that summer programs should be and are more relaxed than the school year, allowing for dropping in and out of the summer session
- a need to care for younger siblings at home
- changes to family plans and vacations
- student dislike of the program, which could be related to bullying or fighting among students
- competing opportunities, which could be related to observing activities of friends and neighbors (who were not in the program) activities.

Relationship of Attendance to Academic Time on Task

In Chapter Two, we described our approach to measuring the hours of instruction that students received during the summer programs, or their "academic time on task." The actual hours of instruction estimated for any particular student varied as a function of days attended and the hours of instruction estimated for their specific classes.

We used the following process to classify attenders as receiving high or low amounts of academic time on task.

- Averaging across classes, we estimated that students received about 1.7 hours of language arts instruction and 1.275 hours of mathematics instruction per day of summer program attendance.
- We then used the previously defined threshold between low and high attendance (20 days), to calculate that, on average, high attenders would have received at

least 34 hours of language arts instruction and at least 25.5 hours of mathematics instruction. We defined these values as the thresholds between low and high academic time on task.

- We estimated each student's academic time on task separately for mathematics and language arts by multiplying their daily attendance by the estimated daily hours of instruction provided in their specific classes.
- We then used the definitions of high and low academic time on task, along with each attending student's estimated academic time on task, to classify them as having received either low or high academic time on task in each subject.

Thus, even though the academic time-on-task categories are defined in a way that is consistent with the attendance categories, considerable variation across classes in the actual instructional time offered means there are high attenders who did not have high academic time on task and vice versa (see Table 3.3).

In both 2013 and 2014, approximately two-thirds of the students who had high academic time on task in language arts also had high academic time on task in mathematics. Averaging across all of the treatment students in summer 2013, 31 percent received high academic time on task in language arts and 28 percent in mathematics (counting only students who attended and excluding no-shows, these numbers increase to 39 and 36 percent, respectively). In summer 2014, 18 percent of all treatment students received high academic time on task in language arts and 20 percent in mathematics (counting only students who attend and excluding no-shows, these numbers increase to 34 and 39 percent, respectively). Approximately 10 percent of all treatment students received high academic time on task in either subject in both summers.

Table 3.3
Numbers of Students Classified as High or Low Attenders and High or Low Academic Time on Task

Year and Characteristic	Mathematics		Language Arts	
	Low Attendance	High Attendance	Low Attendance	High Attendance
Summer 2013				
Low academic time on task	848	770	841	682
High academic time on task	81	815	88	903
Summer 2014				
Low academic time on task	623	384	654	432
High academic time on task	36	609	5	561

District Attempts to Increase Attendance

Districts made substantial efforts to promote strong attendance, as shown in Table 3.4. These activities align with the principles that the advocacy organization Attendance Works highlights as successful strategies.[8] These are to:

- **Recognize and reward good, not perfect, attendance.** Districts did this by offering raffles and small prizes to students based on attendance (e.g., attending four out of five days of the week).
- **Educate parents about the effect of good attendance.** Districts did not engage in direct education, but they did communicate the expectation that students attend the summer program (and not skip weeks because of a family vacation or a competing camp). And they did try to create a warm, welcoming, fun environment that would serve as a magnet for children and to parents.
- **Track student-level longitudinal attendance data** to identify which students are chronically absent. Most districts did this during the experiment, placing calls to parents of absent students.
- **Provide personalized early outreach.** Especially in spring 2013, districts expended substantial effort reaching out to admitted students to encourage them to show up for the program. In one district, teachers wrote personalized notes to

Table 3.4
Activities to Boost Daily Attendance in Summers 2013 and 2014

Attendance-Boosting Activities	District				
	A	B	C	D	E
Establishing stand-alone attendance taking tool to avoid delays and inaccuracies in district student information systems	2013	2013 2014		2014	
Establishing an attendance policy (could lose seat in program if missing more than X days)		2013 2014			2013 2014
Placing calls home daily for absent students (at least in policy, if not always in practice)	2013 2014	2013 2014	2013 2014	2013 2014	2013 2014
Offering ongoing student incentives such as end-of-week raffle or ice cream social based on attendance	2013 2014	2013 2014		2013 2014	2013 2014
Offering end-of-program incentives based on attendance record (e.g., field trip, printed awards)		2013 2014	2014		2013 2014
Placing adult monitors on student busses to call parents to notify them of impending bus arrival or to call absent students		2014			
Offering gifts to parents based on student attendance (e.g., gift cards, movie tickets)			2014		
Holding a culminating performance and inviting families		2013 2014 (some)	2013 2014		2013 2014

---

8   See the "What Works" web page (Attendance Works, 2015) for more detail.

students encouraging them to come to the program and sent those notes home in backpacks. In another, a nonprofit organization conducted home visits. In a third, community-based organizations created videos and slide shows to play for students in in-school information sessions and prior student graduates testified to the fun of the program as a way to excite students to come.

- **Develop program responses to known barriers to attendance.** For the experiment, the districts hosted free, full-day programs to address parents' need for affordable child care. To get students excited to come, districts actively marketed the programs as engaging camps rather than remedial academic work. Finally, districts offered free busing, since transportation might otherwise have been a substantial barrier.

Unfortunately, prior research does not indicate which activities are most effective. There is modest research evidence that incentives, especially to parents, can boost summer program attendance. Our research team conducted an experiment in one district in summer 2011, where the combination of parental gift cards and goody-bag prizes awarded to students who attended four out of five days in a given week increased attendance by 5 percentage points over that district's control group mean of 57 percent. Parental incentives appeared to drive this effect, although the incentives were only effective for students who already had moderate to high attendance rates (Martorell et al., 2016). This finding is consistent with a study of an incentive for students to read books over the summer (Guryan, Kim, and Park, 2015), which found the incentives were only effective for motivated students (as measured by baseline surveys), and the use of incentives actually widened the achievement gap between motivated and unmotivated students. Anecdotally, summer program leaders indicated that their most frequent attendance-boosting activity—phone calls home—helped somewhat in the first week but had no measurable effect thereafter and were quite time-consuming. Instead, some believed that engaging enrichment activities and small weekly incentives (e.g., an ice cream party for strong attendance) helped boost ongoing student attendance.

The one policy lever we identified as having a large effect on attendance rates was making the summer program mandatory rather than voluntary. The ADA in one district in summer 2012 was 83 percent when the large majority of the enrolled students were at threat of grade retention and the summer program was mandatory if these students wanted to be considered for promotion. By contrast, the ADA for the study cohort in this same district was 70 percent in summer 2013; students in the study cohort were not at threat of grade retention.

Conclusions on Attendance

The extensive attendance data collected for this study, and the analyses we were able to conduct with the data, offer new insights into voluntary district-led summer learning programs. For example, district leaders should expect a no-show rate of about 20 to 30 percent for a voluntary summer program for students of this age and should expect that approximately half of students will return from one summer to the next. Districts should also expect that the students who do attend will typically show up 75 percent of summer program days and that 60 percent of attending students will attend at high rates. If districts lack their own historical data, knowing these patterns will help program leaders budget for summer programs; dividing the anticipated number of students present by the desired class sizes will help them determine how many teachers to hire.

Based on anecdotal evidence as well as survey data, we speculate that there are several reasons for low attendance. A more relaxed attitude about summer programs relative to the school year may lend itself to students dropping in and out of the program. The same students who attended 96 percent of the school year, for example, attended 74 percent of the summer session. Infrequent attenders also might have been swayed to participate in other activities by neighbors or friends who were not attending the program. Family vacations and the need for students to provide child care for siblings also reduce attendance during the voluntary summer programs in ways that are not likely during the mandatory school year. And some students stopped attending in the course of the summer. They may have encountered bullying or teasing during the program or did not enjoy it for other reasons.

In examining the characteristics of students who participated at different levels, we found no difference between no-shows and attenders. However, across the entire sample we find that, relative to low attenders, high attenders had lower rates of eligibility for free or reduced-price meals, higher attendance rates the prior school year, and higher prior achievement. The racial and ethnic makeup of the two groups also differed, with the high-attendance group having more African-Americans and Asians and fewer Hispanics than the low-attendance group. Program leaders may want to keep these differences in mind as they develop strategies to boost attendance rates. However, we did observe that it was challenging for the districts in this study to improve ADA rates across summers. Districts with lower levels of attendance made many efforts to improve ADA, with limited effect.

Finally, this attendance analysis is at the heart of the correlational analysis we present in Chapter Five. Because we have reliable information about how often students were present in the classroom and estimates of how much classroom time was spent on academics, we can assess the effects of both attendance and academic time on task on student outcomes.

CHAPTER FOUR

Outcomes After One and Two Summers of Programming: Causal Findings

In this chapter, we present results that arise directly from the randomized controlled trial and thus provide strong evidence on causal relationships between the summer program and outcomes. As described in the introduction, third-grade students were recruited to the program in spring 2013 and randomized into treatment and control groups. Students assigned to the treatment group were accepted into two summers of programming: summer 2013 and summer 2014. The analyses presented in this chapter compare the outcomes of all students who were randomly admitted to two summers of programming with the outcomes of all students who were randomly assigned to the control group, regardless of whether the students actually attended. As such, these estimates represent the impact of *offering* a summer learning program, or the "intent to treat" (ITT) effect.[1] Importantly, because many students who were offered the summer programs did not show up or had poor attendance (and some who were assigned to the control group did attend), these estimates are smaller than the effects experienced by students who attended regularly.[2] (Chapter Five investigates the effects for students who attended; those correlational estimates are less rigorous than the causal estimates presented in this chapter.) In order to protect against finding spurious positive effects, we performed multiple hypothesis test corrections for all confirmatory causal analyses.

In the ensuing sections, we report findings for the following academic, social-emotional, and behavioral outcomes and discuss them in relation to the prior literature on summer program effectiveness:

- mathematics achievement measured by test scores
- language arts achievement measured by test scores

---

[1] Although *Ready for Fall?* (McCombs et al., 2014) reported the estimated effect of "treatment on the treated," technical requirements of that analysis limit its usefulness for examining outcomes after the second summer.

[2] In fact, as discussed in Chapter Three, 21 percent of applicants who were offered the two-summer opportunity did not attend in 2013, and 48 percent did not attend in 2014. While the no-show rate in 2013 was consistent with our expectations, the no-show rate in 2014 was greater than anticipated. All else being equal, low participation adversely affects the average effect across all treatment group students and, consequently, the ability to detect a statistically significant effect.

- mathematics course grades
- language arts course grades
- social-emotional competencies reported by teachers using the DESSA-RRE
- school-year suspension rates
- school-year attendance rates.

Students from all five of the participating districts contributed to the results we report here and in Chapter Five. The study was not designed to have sufficient statistical power to detect effects within districts, nor to detect differential district contributions to the overall results. However, we also acknowledge that the summer programs operated in specific contexts and were enacted by unique groups of administrators, teachers, and students. Because of this, it would be reasonable to suppose that there was variation in the effectiveness of individual programs or that districts contributed differentially to the estimation of the overall program effect. We did explore these questions by estimating district-specific effects and testing the results for evidence of heterogeneity.[3] We found that there is not evidence of meaningful variation in the effectiveness of the individual programs. Based on this, we conclude that all the districts contributed toward the results we highlight in this chapter.

Full details of our statistical models are available in online Appendix E. Further details about the outcomes presented here, including all of the numeric estimates and standard errors, are included in online Appendix F. In all analyses, we controlled for the available information about student baseline characteristics including prior achievement, socioeconomic status, race and ethnicity, gender, special education status, and ELL status.

Overall Findings

We found a general trend of positive program effects for nearly all measured outcomes (the only exception is school-year attendance in 2014–2015). However, the only statistically significant outcome was improved mathematics achievement in fall 2013. Figure 4.1 presents these findings, including outcomes after one summer of programming (2013) and outcomes after both summers. The table highlights statistically significant results with green bars and uses gray for those that are not statistically significant. In all cases, the horizontal length of the bar represents the magnitude of the program effect estimate. We begin by discussing the effects of one summer of programming (2013) in the near term (fall 2013) and longer term (spring 2014). Then we consider the effects of two summers of programming on near-term and longer-term outcomes.

---

[3] Although these district-specific effects are not reported here, we did count them when applying multiple hypothesis test corrections.

Figure 4.1
Causal Effects of Summer Learning Programs on Measured Outcomes for All Treatment Group Students Relative to the Control Group Students

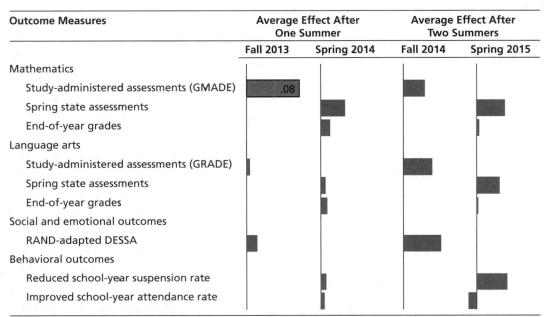

Outcome Measures	Average Effect After One Summer		Average Effect After Two Summers	
	Fall 2013	Spring 2014	Fall 2014	Spring 2015
Mathematics				
Study-administered assessments (GMADE)	.08			
Spring state assessments				
End-of-year grades				
Language arts				
Study-administered assessments (GRADE)				
Spring state assessments				
End-of-year grades				
Social and emotional outcomes				
RAND-adapted DESSA				
Behavioral outcomes				
Reduced school-year suspension rate				
Improved school-year attendance rate				

NOTES: Horizontal length of the bar represents the magnitude of the program effect estimate, with the vertical line representing zero. Green indicates statistically significant after correction for multiple hypothesis tests. All models control for student baseline characteristics, including prior mathematics and ELA achievement, prior attendance and suspensions, poverty, race, gender, and classification as an English learner or a special education student. Blanks indicate data were not available for the particular outcome and time point.
RAND RR1557-4.1

Effects of One Summer of Programming

As mentioned above, the only statistically significant outcome of the 2013 summer programs was a modest near-term effect in mathematics achievement, which was 0.08.[4] As a way of interpreting the magnitude of this effect, we benchmark 0.08 against the size of the typical year-to-year gain that is observed on mathematics assessments similar to the GMADE used in the study. A report synthesizing typical calendar-year gains in mathematics for students of the same age as those in the study found an average effect of 0.52 (Lipsey et al., 2012). By that benchmark, students in the treatment group experienced an advantage over the control group that amounts to 15 percent of typical annual gains. Other evaluations of voluntary summer learning programs have shown near-term boosts in mathematics achievement as well (e.g., Snipes et al., 2015), while others have found no effects (e.g., Somers et al., 2015).

---

[4] McCombs et al. (2014) presented an ITT estimate of 0.09. Since that publication, we gained access to students' school-year attendance data. When we added that data as a covariate, the ITT estimate decreased slightly, to 0.08.

The observed near-term mathematics effects either fade over time, or end-of-year grades and state assessments were not sensitive to the program effects. The fall 2014 results provide useful information that can help us understand the persistence of program effects. The second-year measures allow us to compare scores on the same assessments administered in fall 2013 and fall 2014. If the effects of the program persisted at a constant rate over time, we would anticipate that the fall 2014 estimates would be similar in magnitude to the fall 2013 estimates. In mathematics, the estimated effect after two years of programming is substantially smaller than the fall 2013 estimate and not statistically significant. This offers evidence that the near-term benefits of program participation after the first summer did not persist at the same level over time.

We found no statistically significant effects of the 2013 program on language arts in either the near term or longer term. However, it is worth noting that, while not statistically significant, there is a discernible pattern of small, positive-effect estimates after one summer. And, while caution should be exercised in interpreting these effects as meaningful, this pattern suggests the possibility that there may be small, positive impacts on students' language arts achievement as measured by assessments or end-of-year grades. In the current study, it is not possible to determine conclusively if these are true benefits or if the positive estimates are because of chance and the program has no effect on language arts outcomes.

The literature on the impact of summer programs on language arts outcomes has been mixed; some evaluations have found impacts while others have not. Three recent randomized controlled trials found statistically significant effects of school-based summer programs that focus on reading (Chaplin and Capizzano, 2006) and reading-at-home programs (Kim, 2006; Kim and White, 2008) for students in the same age range as in the study. These studies did not make adjustments for multiple hypothesis testing. Other experimental evaluations of read-at-home programs found no statistically significant effects in reading (Kim, 2004; Kim and Guryan, 2010; Wilkins et al., 2012; White et al., 2014). Some recent studies suggest that the planned hours and duration of the program may not have been sufficient to improve reading outcomes. One study found that out-of-school-time reading programs between 44 hours and 84 hours in length had positive effects on reading outcomes, but programs offering fewer than 44 hours did not result in benefits (Lauer et al., 2006). In the study, in 2014, planned hours of language arts instruction ranged from 38 hours to 48 hours, depending upon the district. Taking into consideration average student attendance and use of classroom time, we estimate that the students in the study actually received an average of only 19 to 29 hours of reading instruction, depending on the program in which they were enrolled.

We did not see a significant impact on social-emotional or behavioral outcomes after one summer program. While the overall trend in all measured effects is positive, these estimates are so small that it is not possible to determine if they are meaningful. It is possible there is no effect of summer program participation on these measures. Only one other rigorous study of summer learning has tracked nonacademic outcomes

(Chapin and Capizzano, 2006), and its authors also did not find statistically significant effects of the program on academic self-perception or social behaviors.

Effects of Two Summers of Programming

In our causal models, we did not observe any effects of the programs after the second summer. The high no-show rates in the second summer pose a challenge in estimating the impact of two years of summer programming. Nearly half of the students who were initially offered a summer program slot did not attend in 2014. All of those students are still considered part of the treatment group in the experimental analyses and factor into the causal estimates of effects on fall 2014 and spring 2015 outcomes. This is an important consideration, as the no-show members of the treatment group can be conceived of as "diluting" the estimation of treatment effects. The higher the no-show rate, the larger the effect of the program (on those who do attend) would have to be in order to be detected. For the same reason, if the effects accumulated in consecutive summers, they would have to accumulate by a substantial amount for us to be able to detect this statistically.

Student Characteristics as Moderators of Treatment Effects

We ran additional analyses to examine whether three specific groups of participants experienced larger or smaller treatment effects than students not in those groups. The groups were ELL, students eligible for free or reduced-price lunch, and students who had the lowest performance on prior achievement tests. These analyses were conducted to test *a priori* hypotheses that certain student groups may benefit from the program more than others. The hypotheses were grounded in prior research suggesting summer programming can help to remediate achievement gaps evident in these subgroups.

The estimated effects for members versus nonmembers of these groups were small, nonsignificant, and inconsistent over time. We conclude that these groups experienced approximately the same effects as other students in the treatment group and that we can rule out differential treatment effects for these groups.

The findings are consistent with Arbreton et al. (2011), which found no relationship between family income and summer program effectiveness. However, other studies have found that lower-income students, or students attending schools with larger shares of lower-income students, were found to have gained more than their higher-income peers in some summer programs (Allington et al., 2010; Kim and Quinn, 2013; White et al., 2014), which is not supported in our sample.

Conclusions from Causal Analyses

We have strong evidence that one summer of the program produced a modest near-term benefit in mathematics in fall 2013. That was the only statistically significant result from our causal analyses, although we did find small positive trends for nearly all of the other outcomes and time points examined. There is no evidence that the near-term benefit in mathematics persisted over time: Whether measured by state assessments or study-administered standardized assessments, the longer-term measures show substantially smaller impacts. There is an extensive body of literature showing that many education interventions show patterns of fadeout: Programs that show strong impacts measured at the end of treatment do not show the same results after more time has elapsed (Schweinhart et al., 2005; Puma et al., 2012; Bailey et al., 2015; Protzko, 2015). In some cases, significant positive effects are found to emerge in adult outcomes years after observing this fade (Schweinhart et al., 2005; Bradshaw et al., 2009; Chetty et al., 2011; Campbell et al., 2014).

We have no clear evidence that offering two summers of programming adds to the benefits that students receive after just one summer in mathematics. Additionally, offering two summers of programming did not show significant effects in reading, social-emotional development, or students' behavior during the school year. However, given the fact that nearly half of the treatment students did not participate in summer programming in the second year, this is not surprising.

In the next chapter, we draw on our implementation data to explore whether programmatic features and students' attendance are related to student outcomes.

CHAPTER FIVE

Factors That Influence Outcomes: Insights from Correlational Analyses

In this chapter, we explore the relationships among attendance, academic time on task, certain implementation features, and student outcomes. We hypothesized that these factors might be related to program effects and could be useful in helping to explain the causal results. These results are important because they provide evidence about the aspects of programming that might influence student outcomes—information that is useful for summer program leaders and administrators.

These analyses are correlational rather than causal (experimental) because we are comparing the entire control group to subsets of the treatment group that were not randomly chosen to be part of those subsets.[1] For that reason, as explained in Chapter One, selection into these groups remains a possibility, and thus the effects estimated by these analyses may be biased. As one example, when we examined the relationship between prior achievement and program attendance, we found some evidence of systematic differences. Students with higher attendance, on average, had higher levels of prior mathematics achievement (measured before the experiment started) than students in the control group. In addition to group differences that are evident in available student variables, there is the potential for differences among groups in these analyses that are not apparent because we do not have variables measuring them (for example, the importance placed on education by family members). To help mitigate potential bias, we controlled for the same broad set of student characteristics as in our causal analyses, including prior academic performance.[2] While we cannot rule out the possibility that unmeasured characteristics caused or contributed to the correlational results described below, we think the sum of evidence makes it likely that the academic results are because of participation in the summer learning program. We are moderately less confident that the social-emotional results are not because of selection bias, because we lack a pretreatment measure of those outcomes for use as a statistical control.

---

[1] We did not apply corrections for multiple hypothesis tests to the correlational analyses reported in this chapter because they are considered exploratory.

[2] Baseline variables included prior achievement scores, eligibility for free or reduced price lunch, race/ethnicity, ELL status, special education status, sex, school year attendance, and school-year suspension.

We examined nine characteristics of summer programs and summer program participation that we hypothesized might affect the summer programs' effects on student outcomes:

1. attendance (or the number of days a student attended the program)
2. academic time on task, which reflects the number of academic instructional hours a student received
3. relative opportunity for individual attention, which combines academic time on task and class size
4. quality of instruction in students' mathematics and language arts classrooms
5. appropriateness of the curriculum, including ratings of pace, clarity, and alignment with student performance levels
6. teacher's prior teaching experiences with the sending or receiving grade level
7. positive instructional climate
8. daily site climate
9. site discipline and order.

These variables are discussed in Chapters Two and Three, and additional details about the definitions of these variables and information about how data were collected are available in online Appendix B. Information about the analytic models used in these analyses is available in online Appendix E.

In the remainder of the chapter, we discuss in detail only those factors that were found to have consistent positive associations with student outcomes across time. These were attendance and academic time on task, which had such associations with multiple outcomes. Another factor, quality of instruction, was found to have consistent positive associations only with language arts outcomes. The other factors did not show consistent associations (positive or negative) with student outcomes across time, and are not discussed here. Complete results are available in online Appendix F.

Effects of Attendance: Results After the First and Second Summer

We expected that summer program attendance would be positively associated both with near-term and long-term student outcomes. Using daily attendance data, we analyzed the relationship between student attendance and program effects and found that increased attendance was associated with positive outcomes across multiple measures. We also examined categories of attendance to see whether higher attendance was associated with greater benefits. As explained in Chapter Three, we split students into three categories of attendance—no-shows (zero days attended), "low" attendance (one to 19 days attended), and "high" attendance (20 or more days attended)—and ran statistical models to compare the outcomes of each of these groups to the control group outcomes.[3] Recall that, in 2013, approximately 21 percent of students were no-shows, 29 percent were low attenders, and 50 percent were high attenders. In 2014, approximately 48 percent were no-shows, 21 percent were low attenders, and 31 percent were high attenders. (For details on how we determined appropriate cut points for low and high attendance, see online Appendix D.)

The results are presented in Figure 5.1. We found that the stronger the attendance, the larger the estimated treatment effects on mathematics, reading, and social-emotional outcomes. Many of these effects are strong enough to be statistically significant, as shown by the green bars. These findings comport with prior research, which have also found a relationship between attendance and positive outcomes (Cooper, Charlton, et al., 2000; Borman, Benson, and Overman, 2005; Borman

Figure 5.1
Correlational Effects of Program Attendance in Most Recent Summer on Assessment Outcomes for Subsets of Treatment Group Students Relative to the Control Group Students

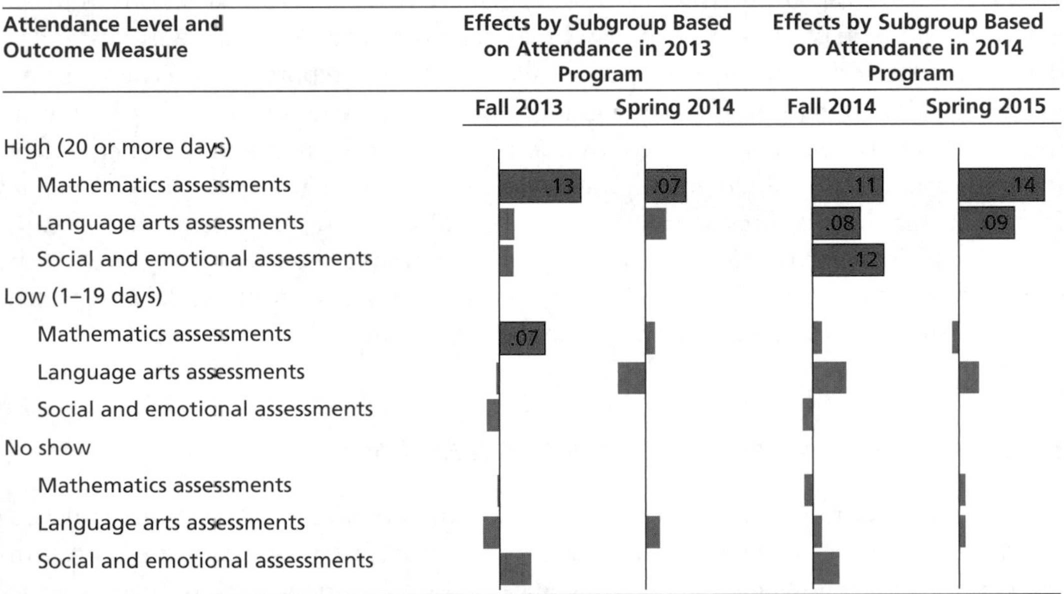

Attendance Level and Outcome Measure	Effects by Subgroup Based on Attendance in 2013 Program		Effects by Subgroup Based on Attendance in 2014 Program	
	Fall 2013	Spring 2014	Fall 2014	Spring 2015
High (20 or more days)				
Mathematics assessments	.13	.07	.11	.14
Language arts assessments			.08	.09
Social and emotional assessments			.12	
Low (1–19 days)				
Mathematics assessments	.07			
Language arts assessments				
Social and emotional assessments				
No show				
Mathematics assessments				
Language arts assessments				
Social and emotional assessments				

NOTES: Horizontal length of the bar represents the magnitude of the program effect estimate, with the vertical line representing zero. Green indicates statistically significant. All models control for student baseline characteristics, including prior mathematics and ELA achievement, prior attendance and suspensions, poverty, race, gender, and classification as an ELL or a special education student. Blanks indicate data were not available for the particular outcome and time point.
RAND RR1557-5.1

---

[3] We attempted a variety of "causal mediation" strategies (including principal stratification, marginal structural models, and prognostic scores), but these methods were not successful in strengthening the rigor of the attendance (or academic time on task) analyses. We were unable to develop a model to predict attendance, underscoring the lack of strong correlations between students' characteristics and attendance.

and Dowling, 2006; McCombs, Pane, et al., 2014). We did not find consistent relationships between attendance and end-of-year grades, school-year attendance, or suspension rates after either summer.

After summer 2013, students with high attendance received a near-term benefit in mathematics (0.13) that was also detected later, in the spring 2014 state assessments (0.07). However, high attenders in 2013 did not receive a significant boost in language arts, social-emotional outcomes, or school-year behaviors.

For students who attended at high rates in summer 2014, we found positive near-term effects of the program in mathematics (0.11) and language arts (0.08) that were also demonstrated on state assessments in spring 2015 (0.14 and 0.09, respectively). Because nearly 80 percent of the students who were high attenders in 2014 were also high attenders in 2013, it is not possible to completely separate the effects of high attendance in the 2014 program from the effects of high attendance in both summers. In fact, the impacts for high attenders in 2014 may be partially because of the cumulative effects of high attendance, an idea that is supported by the two-year attendance results presented in the next section.

Again, as a way to interpret the magnitude of these positive associations in mathematics and language arts, we can benchmark against normative expectations for academic growth in these subjects (Lipsey et al., 2012). That report found typical spring-to-spring gains in math of 0.52 from grades three to four and 0.56 from grades four to five. Of the mathematics results reported in Figure 5.1, the estimated treatment effects for high attenders versus control group students represent between 13 percent and 25 percent of those annual gains.[4] Lipsey et al. (2012) describe corresponding gains of 0.36 and 0.40 in reading. Of the language arts results reported in Figure 5.1, the estimated treatment effects for high attenders versus control group students represent between 20 percent and 23 percent of those annual gains.

Effects of Two Consecutive Years of Attendance

Using attendance information for two years, we compare the effects on students attending the program in summer 1 only, attending in summer 2 only, attending both summers, and having consecutive high attendance in both summers. Each of these analyses divides the treatment group into two subgroups—those who met the specified attendance criterion and the rest of the treatment group—and compares these groups' outcomes with the control group. Of the students in the treatment group, approximately one-third of the students attended in 2013 only; 6 percent of the students attended in

---

[4]   Lipsey et al. (2012) does not define two-year benchmarks. Because of this, we are benchmarking against the one-year benchmarks, even though it is not possible to determine when summer learning effects accrued for the fall 2014 and spring 2015 outcomes. For fall 2013 and spring 2014, we benchmark against grades three to four, and for fall 2014 and spring 2015, we benchmark against grades four to five.

2014 only; and half of the students attended both summers. Approximately 29 percent of treatment students were high attenders in both summers. The small percentage of students attending only in summer 2014 further limits our ability to disaggregate this group and investigate the effects of the program on students who only attended in 2014 and were high attenders that summer.

Figure 5.2 presents the results from these analyses. Students who only attended in summer 2013 did not perform better than the control group on any of these outcomes after the second summer. In contrast, students who attended both summers performed better than control group students in mathematics (0.09) and language arts (0.08) in fall 2014. These effects also persist over time—positive gains on fall 2014 assessments were also demonstrated on spring 2015 assessments (0.08 in mathematics and 0.07 in language arts). Students who were consecutive high attenders also performed better than control group students in fall 2014 in mathematics (0.10) and language arts (0.12), and these effects persisted through spring 2015.

Figure 5.2
Correlational Effects of Attending Two Years of Summer Programing on Assessment Outcomes for Subsets of Treatment Group Students Relative to the Control Group Students

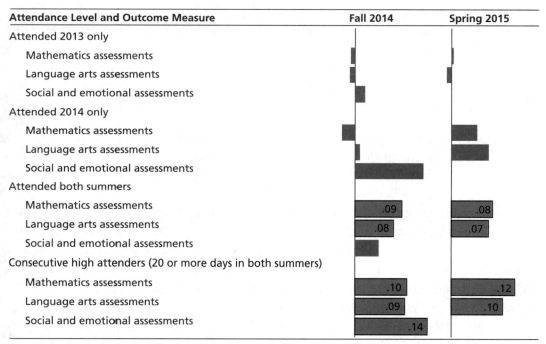

NOTES: Horizontal length of the bar represents the magnitude of the program effect estimate, with the vertical line representing zero. Green indicates statistically significant. All models control for student baseline characteristics, including prior mathematics and ELA achievement, prior attendance and suspensions, poverty, race, gender, and classification as an ELL or a special education student. Blanks indicate data were not available for the particular outcome and time point.
RAND *RR1557-5.2*

Significant impacts on social-emotional outcomes also emerge for students after the second summer. Students who had high attendance in both summers scored higher on DESSA-RRE than their control group peers (0.14). This relationship is not significant for students who attended both summers (when combining high and low attenders). Unlike the mathematics and language arts analyses, where we were able to explore selection bias using prior achievement, we were unable to similarly control for selection bias for the social-emotional outcomes because there are no available baseline (pretreatment) measures. Thus, we cannot rule out the possibility that these results are driven by selection—in particular, it may be the case that students who had high attendance in both summers systematically exhibited more positive social-emotional behaviors prior to program participation.

It is clear that higher levels of attendance in the second summer and consecutive years of high attendance show positive and persistent effects on language arts and mathematics outcomes relative to students in the control groups (as shown in Figure 5.2). These represent between 14 percent and 21 percent of typical annual gains in mathematics, and 17 percent and 25 percent of the typical annual gains in reading (Lipsey et al., 2012). However, we cannot be certain whether these benefits come from cumulative program exposure, improved programming in the second summer, uncontrolled selection bias, or a combination of these factors. Based on the pattern of results and our knowledge of program implementation, we hypothesize that, for the academic outcomes, it is a combination of cumulative program benefits and improved programming during the second summer.

Effects of Academic Time on Task

As previously discussed, prior research has shown that while attendance is necessary for students to benefit from summer programs, it is not sufficient. It is just as important that classroom time is being used for academic instruction and that students are engaged in learning when they are in attendance.

We examined the relationship between academic time on task and academic outcomes (including assessments and end-of-year grades) in both mathematics and language arts. We do not report the results for grades here because they did not show consistent effects over time. Figure 5.3 presents the associations between academic time on task and academic assessments. Results for four different categories are presented in this figure, three of which characterize academic time on task in a single summer (either summer 2013 or summer 2014) and one of which characterizes academic time on task across both summers. The single-summer categories include no-shows, low academic time on task, and high academic time on task. For example, the estimated effect of high academic time on task for fall 2013 mathematics assessments (with a value of 0.16) indicates that students who received at least 25.5 hours of instruction in math-

Figure 5.3
Correlational Effects of Academic Time on Task on Academic Outcomes for Subsets of Treatment Group Students Relative to the Control Group Students

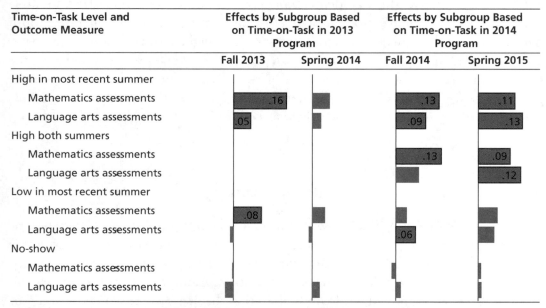

Time-on-Task Level and Outcome Measure	Effects by Subgroup Based on Time-on-Task in 2013 Program		Effects by Subgroup Based on Time-on-Task in 2014 Program	
	Fall 2013	Spring 2014	Fall 2014	Spring 2015
High in most recent summer				
Mathematics assessments	.16		.13	.11
Language arts assessments	.05		.09	.13
High both summers				
Mathematics assessments			.13	.09
Language arts assessments				.12
Low in most recent summer				
Mathematics assessments	.08			
Language arts assessments			.06	
No-show				
Mathematics assessments				
Language arts assessments				

NOTES: Horizontal length of the bar represents the magnitude of the program effect estimate, with the vertical line representing zero. Green indicates statistically significant. All models control for student baseline characteristics, including prior mathematics and ELA achievement, prior attendance and suspensions, poverty, race, gender, and classification as an ELL or a special education student. Blanks indicate data were not available for the particular outcome and time point. High academic time-on-task levels are 25.5 or more hours in mathematics, and 34 or more hours in language arts. Low academic time-on-task levels are less than 25.5 hours in mathematics, and less than 34 hours in language arts.
RAND RR1557-5.3

ematics in summer 2013 performed significantly better than control group students on the fall 2013 mathematics assessment. Likewise, the estimated effect of high academic time on task for fall 2014 mathematics assessments (with a value of 0.13) indicates that students who received at least 25.5 hours of instruction in mathematics in summer 2014 performed significantly better than control group students on this test. For the sake of interpretation, the estimates shown in Figure 5.3 represent between 15 percent and 21 percent of typical annual gains in mathematics, and 13 percent and 33 percent of typical annual gains in reading (Lipsey et al., 2012).

We found that greater academic time on task was associated with larger estimated treatment effects relative to control students, as measured by standardized assessments. For summer 2013, students who received high academic time on task showed significant treatment effects on mathematics (0.16) and language arts (0.05) outcomes in the fall. Students who received lower levels of time on task in mathematics also had a significant fall treatment effect (0.08), although it was smaller than the effect for their peers in the higher academic time on task group. None of the estimated treatment effects for these groups and subjects were statistically significant in spring 2014.

We found that students who had high academic time on task in summer 2014 and those who received high academic time on task in both summers (2013 and 2014) experienced positive effects on the fall 2014 and spring 2015 assessments in both mathematics and language arts, and seven of these eight estimates were significant. As with attendance results, we hypothesize that the advantages we observed after the second summer represent a combination of cumulative exposure over two summers and improved programming in the second summer. More than half of the students who had high academic time on task in summer 2014 also had high academic time on task in summer 2013.

Effect of Language Arts Instructional Quality

Finally, we examined the link between instructional quality and student outcomes. As described in Chapter Two, our measure focused on clear and purposeful instruction with on-task teachers and students and with teachers ensuring that each student understood the material taught during the observed lesson. Along with the other implementation features we examined, we hypothesized that the quality of instruction would be related to students' outcomes. We found consistent positive associations between the quality of language arts instruction and language arts achievement, shown in Figure 5.4. The near-term effect of instructional quality was statistically significant. These positive trends persisted through the spring and fall 2014, although they were no longer significant.

Figure 5.4
Correlational Effects for Students Receiving High-Quality Language Arts Instruction Relative to the Control Group Students

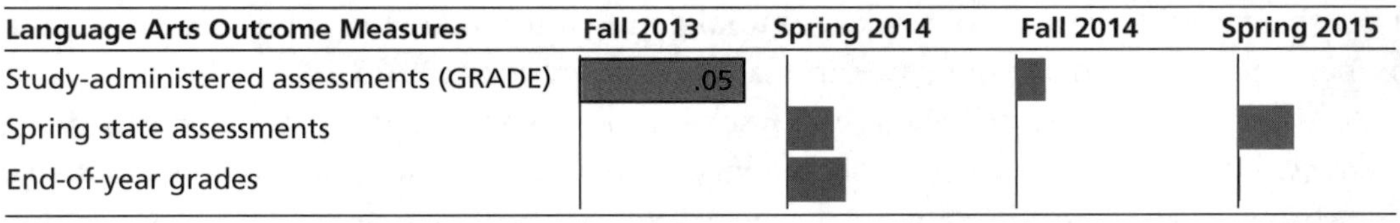

Language Arts Outcome Measures	Fall 2013	Spring 2014	Fall 2014	Spring 2015
Study-administered assessments (GRADE)	.05		▮	
Spring state assessments		▮		▮
End-of-year grades		▮		

NOTES: Horizontal length of the bar represents the magnitude of the program effect estimate, with the vertical line representing zero. Green indicates statistically significant. All models control for student baseline characteristics, including prior mathematics and ELA achievement, prior attendance and suspensions, poverty, race, gender, and classification as an ELL or a special education student. Blanks indicate data were not available for the particular outcome and time point.

RAND *RR1557-5.4*

Conclusions from Correlational Analyses

We found that attendance and estimated academic time on task were positively related to outcomes. After one summer of programming, students with high rates of attendance had higher near-term achievement in mathematics relative to control students. This association persisted into the spring. Students experiencing high academic time on task the first summer outperformed control students on fall 2013 assessments in both language arts and mathematics, although we did not see that benefit persist into the spring.

Although there was consistency in the attendance and academic time on task results with regard to mathematics achievement, this was less true for language arts. Specifically, while students with high academic time on task and those who received higher quality instruction in 2013 received a significant near-term boost in language arts; students who were high attenders in 2013 did not. This may indicate that providing adequate opportunities for academic time on task (and protecting those opportunities from disruption) and ensuring quality instruction in language arts is as important as ensuring that students attend the program.

After summer 2014, students who had attended both summer programs, attended at high rates for both summers, attended at high rates in summer 2014, experienced high academic time on task in summer 2014, or some combination thereof had higher near-term language arts and mathematics achievement relative to control students. These associations persisted through the school year as indicated by the spring 2015 state assessments. We also found a positive association between attendance and scores on the DESSA-RRE, our measure of social-emotional competencies that examined self-regulation and self-motivation (we did not measure the link between time on task and social-emotional competencies because there was not classroom time explicitly devoted to those competencies as there was for mathematics and language arts).

Although these results are correlational, we gain confidence in them by viewing them in the context of the causal experimental results. First, it makes sense that the consistent pattern of positive causal estimates (while mostly not statistically significant) for mathematics, language arts, and social-emotional competencies (which were reported in Chapter Four) accrued to the students who actually attended the program. More formally, the correlational estimates for attenders reported in this chapter are in plausible numeric ranges, given the causal estimates.[5] We use a rich set of characteris-

---

[5]   Full analytic models used for attendance and academic time on task are detailed in online Appendix E and are based on the random-effects model specifications used to estimate ITT effects. As another method to explore the robustness of these correlational estimates, we calculated the weighted sum of the correlational treatment estimates for low and high attenders the first year. Together, these students comprise "the treated" students in first-year causal models that estimate the effect of "treatment on the treated" (the results of which are reported in online Appendix F). The weighted sum of the correlational estimates closely reproduce the estimated causal effects of treatment on the treated, consistent with a lack of bias in the first-year correlational treatment effect estimates.

tics as statistical controls to reduce the potential for selection bias in these analyses. We are less certain that we adequately controlled for students' social-emotional competencies in our modeling because of the lack of an aligned baseline measure.

We hypothesize that the positive effects after the second summer for consecutive attenders, high attenders, and students with high academic time on task reflect a combination of cumulative program exposure and improved programming in the second summer. Because the majority of students who were high attenders in 2014 (and had high academic time on task in 2014) also were high attenders in 2013 (and had high academic time on task in 2013), we cannot determine whether cumulative attendance or improved programming was more influential.

Finally, we found consistent positive associations between the quality of instruction and language arts achievement; however, only the 2013 near-term effect of instructional quality on reading achievement was statistically significant. It may be that language arts instruction is more sensitive to quality than mathematics instruction. These positive estimates also exist at three other time points through spring 2015 but are not statistically significant.

None of the other correlations we tested produced a consistent pattern of results we judged noteworthy. The full results are shown in online Appendix F.

CHAPTER SIX

Overall Conclusions and Implications

This study tests whether voluntary district-led summer programs of five to six weeks' duration that include academics and enrichment activities benefit low-income upper-elementary students. It addresses an important policy question because recent research confirms that low-income students fall behind their higher-income peers academically during the summer. The study is particularly compelling because it includes five different programs in five states and examines multiple outcomes over time, including those that are rarely measured, such as social-emotional outcomes and school-year behavior. The study also adds to our knowledge of attendance in voluntary programs.

Implementation Findings

Programs Implemented Common Features with Fidelity but Instructional Quality Varied Within and Across Sites

Program leaders implemented with fidelity the common features requested of them to participate in this study: Program leaders offered at least five weeks of free and voluntary programs with transportation and meals provided at no cost and offering at least three scheduled hours of academics a day taught by certified teachers to small classes of students.

It is easier to determine this fidelity to basic program features than to determine the quality of programming. We did see variation in quality across, and even within, sites as we observed students throughout each day. In each of the program sites, we observed challenges as well as several positive aspects of the programs. When we consider our observations across all of the sites, common instructional challenges included developing curricula that met the needs of all students and, similarly, striving to ensure that all students understood the presented material in each classroom. However, in almost all of the classrooms we observed, teachers and students were on-task, with teachers providing clear instruction. The teachers reported that they enjoyed teaching in the programs, the sites were well managed, and logistics ran smoothly. Students had opportunities to participate in, and enjoyed, enrichment activities designed to be fun and engaging, and many students had clearly developed strong relationships with adults working in the programs.

Attendance Findings

Student Participation Was Weaker in the Second Summer

Demand for summer programming was strong, as evidenced by each district exceeding enrollment targets when they recruited the students in spring 2013. Districts made considerable efforts to communicate with parents and students about the importance of attending the program and a higher proportion of students (about 80 percent) did come to the program in 2013 than we had observed in prior summers. This suggests that districts can improve on no-show rates, but not eliminate them completely. And we found no differences based on observable characteristics (e.g., achievement, race/ethnicity, family income) between students who did not show up and students who chose to attend.

In contrast to the 20-percent no-show rate in 2013, nearly half did not show up for the summer 2014 program. To understand this increase, it is important to remember that it includes students who had left the district—about 11 percent of the total study sample. It also represents the nonparticipation rate of students who were invited 14 months earlier to attend the program in both summer 2013 and summer 2014. This time lag increased the possibility that students made other plans for the second summer. Because of this decline in participation from one summer to the next, both the low attenders and the high attenders in 2014 were a smaller proportion of the treatment group than in the first summer. That fact influenced the estimates of the impacts of the program on the treatment group.

Students Who Participated Attended About 75 percent of the Time

It proved more challenging for program leaders to increase ADA rates. Because attending the five- to six-week summer programs was voluntary, we expected that not all students who had applied would attend, and that those who attended the programs would do so at rates lower than during the mandatory school year. Indeed, despite multiple and varied efforts to improve attendance rates across four summers (2011–2014), ADA rates remained relatively consistent. Each summer, on average, students who attended came about 75 percent of the time. But this average disguises substantive variation by district. Depending on the district, ADA varied from a low of 60 percent in one district to a high of 80 percent in another—these district-specific rates also remained constant over the four-year period. In each district, attendance rates peaked in the first week and declined over the course of the summer, suggesting that some students became less engaged over time.

Although summer learning experts have recommended aiming for an ADA rate of 85 percent, the study calls into question the feasibility of that goal for programs similar to those we studied. Even the districts with the highest ADA rates did not meet this goal despite removing potential barriers to participation by offering full-day programming at no cost to families, free transportation, and meals.

Averaging across all districts, in each summer, about 60 percent of students who participated in the program were high attenders, meaning that they attended at least 20 days in a summer. Individual districts also varied widely in the proportion of participating students who were high attenders—ranging in summer 2013 from a low of 52 percent to a high of 85 percent.

Causal Findings on Program Effects

Our causal estimates compare the outcomes of all students who were randomly admitted to two summers of programming with the outcomes of all students who were randomly assigned to the control group, regardless of whether the students actually attended. As such, these estimates represent the impact of *offering* a summer learning program. Importantly, because many students who were offered the summer programs did not show up, particularly in the second summer, or had poor attendance (and a few who were assigned to the control group did attend), these estimates are smaller than the effects experienced by students who did attend regularly.

Modest Near-Term Benefit in Mathematics, Dissipated by the Next Fall

We have strong evidence that one summer of the program produced a modest near-term benefit (measured in fall 2013) in mathematics. The standardized average effect of offering the program was 0.08 and was statistically significant. To put this finding in context, studies of school-year achievement of students the same age using mathematics assessments similar to ours found annual achievement gains of 0.52 (Lipsey et al., 2012). By that benchmark, students in the treatment group experienced a boost relative to the control group of about 15 percent of that annual gain. A five-week summer program is about 10 percent of a calendar year and 15 percent of a school year. Other evaluations of voluntary summer learning programs have shown near-term boosts in mathematics achievement as well (e.g., Snipes et al., 2015) while others have found no effects (e.g., Somers et al., 2015).

However, we found no evidence that the mathematics benefit persisted over time. Whether measured by state assessments in the spring or the standardized assessment we readministered in the subsequent fall, the longer-term effects of the program are positive but much smaller and statistically insignificant. In contrast, prior evaluations of mandatory summer programs have found effects in the following spring (e.g., Jacob and Lefgren, 2004; Matsudaira, 2008). It may be that those stronger outcomes are because of higher student attendance rates when the programs are required for promotion to the next grade level.

Our causal modeling found no statistically significant impacts from one summer program for treatment group students in language arts outcomes, in either the near term or longer term. The literature regarding summer program effects on language arts for students at this grade level shows mixed results: Some researchers find benefits while others do not. It could be that planned hours and duration in the programs we studied may not have been sufficient to improve reading outcomes. One study found that out-of-school-time reading programs between 44 hours and 84 hours in length had the largest effects on reading outcomes, but programs offering fewer than 44 hours did not result in positive benefits (Lauer et al., 2006). In this study, planned hours of language arts instruction ranged from 39 hours to 47 hours, depending upon the district.

Based on our causal analyses, we found no significant effects of the program for treatment group students on social-emotional outcomes, school-year grades, school-year attendance, school-year suspension rates, or spring state assessment scores.

Students who had ELL status, were eligible for free or reduced-price lunch, or had the lowest performance on prior achievement tests experienced approximately the same effects as other students in the treatment group. These students benefited no more, and no less, than the other treatment students.

No Causal Evidence That Two Summers of Programming Provided Benefits

We found no significant effects from offering two summers of programming in the causal analysis. The low participation rate in the second summer—with only 52 percent of treatment students attending—hindered our ability to detect a significant treatment effect. The higher the no-show rate, the larger the effect of the program would have to be in order to be detected. Even if the impacts accumulated from consecutive summers, the accumulation would have had to be substantial for us to detect it statistically, given the high no-show rate in the second summer.

Taken together, the causal results show positive effects across nearly all measures and time points, although they are too slight to be statistically significant (except for mathematics performance after one summer). The consistency of these trends might suggest that the programs may confer some small benefits that could not be detected in this experiment or that the programs truly had minimal to no effect on the outcomes. We generally conclude that we have no evidence of causal impacts except for the near-term mathematics estimate after the first summer.

Correlational Findings on Program Effects

These analyses are correlational (exploratory) rather than causal (experimental) because they compare the control group students to subsets of the treatment group that were not randomly chosen. For that reason, selection bias remains a possibility. To help mitigate potential bias, we controlled for the same broad set of student characteristics as in the causal analyses, including prior academic performance. While we cannot rule out the possibility that unmeasured characteristics caused or contributed to the correlational results described below, we think the sum of evidence makes it likely that the academic results are because of participation in the summer learning program. We are moderately less confident that the social-emotional results are not because of selection bias, because we lack a pretreatment measure of those outcomes for use as a statistical control.

Promising Evidence That High Attendance in One Summer Led to Mathematics Benefits That Persisted into the Following Spring

After summer 2013, students with high attendance received a near-term benefit in mathematics (0.13, or 25 percent of the average annual gain) that persisted through the school year as demonstrated on the spring 2014 state assessments (0.07, or 13 percent of the expected annual gain). We did not find this significant persistence of effects for all treatment students. It could be that the higher levels of attendance conferred sufficient benefits to enable these students to maintain an advantage over the control group during the school year.

Promising Evidence That High Attendance in the Second Summer Led to Mathematics and Language Arts Benefits That Persisted

After summer 2014, students who attended at high rates saw near-term positive effects on the measures of mathematics (0.11) and language arts achievement (0.08), which persisted through the school year based on results of state assessments in spring 2015 (0.14 in mathematics and 0.09 in language arts).

These positive academic outcomes most likely reflect a combination of cumulative program exposure over the course of two summers and improved quality of programming in the second summer, particularly in language arts (we did note improvements in the language arts curriculum in the second summer). Because the majority of students who were high attenders in 2014 were also high attenders in 2013, we cannot isolate whether the effects derive from cumulative attendance, program improvements in the second summer, or both. These results are consistent with the literature on consecutive summers of programming. One such study reported positive effects only for those children who participated for at least two summers with attendance rates of greater than 39 percent (Borman and Dowling, 2006). Another study of a books-at-home intervention found benefits only at the end of the third consecutive summer (Allington et al., 2010).

Promising Evidence That High Attenders in the Second Summer Benefited in Terms of Social-Emotional Outcomes

We also found a positive benefit for high attenders on the near-term measure of social-emotional competencies (0.12), the DESSA-RRE, which measured self-regulation and self-motivation. (We do not have a long-term measure for these effects.) Unlike the mathematics and language arts analyses where we were able to help control for selection bias using prior achievement variables in our models, we were unable to similarly control for baseline (pretreatment) social-emotional skills because no such measures were available.

Promising Evidence That High Academic Time on Task Led to Benefits That Tended to Persist

Besides attendance data, we estimated the class time that instructors spent teaching the academic material, based on classroom observations. To calculate how much instruction each student received, we considered their attendance and estimates of academic time on task from the classroom observations we conducted on a small sample of classes. These calculations varied by district: For example, in the district with lowest ADA rates in 2014, the average student received about 19 hours of language arts instruction instead of the planned 38 hours. That same summer, in the district with the highest ADA rates, the average student received about 33 hours of language arts instruction, instead of the 47 hours that were planned.

In both mathematics and language arts, outcomes for students with high academic time on task were consistently positive—and often significant—compared with control students. The amount of academic time on task necessary to be defined as high was 34 hours of language arts instruction and about 25 hours of mathematics instruction. Overall, in summer 2013 and 2014, approximately one-third of attending students received high academic time on task in language arts or mathematics during the summer program.

In summer 2013, students who received high levels of academic time on task received a positive benefit in mathematics that persisted on the spring assessments relative to control students. Students with high academic time on task in language arts in summer 2013 also received a significant near-term benefit from the program. However, this effect size was relatively small (0.05), and no significant effect was detected on the state assessment the following spring. Interestingly, high attenders (as opposed to students with high academic time on task) in 2013 did *not* receive a significant near-term boost in language arts. This finding suggests that the amount of instructional time is particularly important in language arts.

In summer 2014, students who received high levels of academic time on task gained significant benefits relative to control students in mathematics (0.13) and language arts (0.09) in the fall and these effects persisted into spring 2015. We again hypothesize that benefits after the second summer are likely a combination of improved programming and cumulative exposure.

Promising Evidence That Students with High-Quality Language Arts Instruction Benefited from the Programs

We found consistent positive associations between the quality of instruction and language arts achievement. The measure of instructional quality focused on clear instruction, on-task behavior, and teachers' ensuring that all students understood the material. The near-term effect of instructional quality, measured in fall 2013 after the first summer, was statistically significant. These positive trends persisted through the spring and fall 2014, although they were no longer significant.

Implications for Summer Program Leaders

The results provide evidence that should be useful for district and community partners who are implementing voluntary summer programs or are considering doing so. For example, we demonstrate that the programs provide near-term benefits in mathematics after a single summer. The evidence of this effect is considered "strong" under the standards set forth in the new ESSA (Sec 8101 (21) (A)). Therefore, a summer learning program like those in this study might be eligible for federal funding under ESSA if the program targets mathematics skills. High-attending students are likely to reap multiple benefits from these programs. These results, considered "promising" under ESSA (which defines *promising* to mean "at least one well-designed and implemented correlational study that controls for selection bias"), might be used to attract federal funding if districts can demonstrate a track record of high attendance in their summer programs.

In addition, our detailed implementation analysis holds lessons for district leaders and other practitioners on how to improve the effectiveness of summer learning programs.

We recommend offering at least five weeks of programming—and preferably six or more—with at least three hours of academics per day. Given the benefits for students who attended at least 20 days, and the average daily attendance rates for these programs, offering six or more weeks of programming should mean that more students would benefit.

We were not able to distinguish whether the strong outcomes of students attending two summers resulted from cumulative attendance or from improved program quality in the second summer. Both appear important. In light of this finding, district leaders should encourage students to attend for consecutive summers. However, the findings give reason to believe that only about half of students offered the program will return for a second summer.

It is important to offer programs of sufficient duration and to ensure that students experience sufficient time on academics when they are in attendance. We observed benefits for students if they had approximately 25 hours of instruction in mathematics and 34 hours in language arts over the course of a summer. These are not "offered" program hours, but the hours received when we take student attendance and the productive use of class time into consideration. One lesson from these findings is the importance of protecting the integrity of the full academic block and refraining from scheduling transitions (such as a lunch break in the middle of an academic block), pulling students out for assemblies, or other activities during academic time.

Promoting consistent and high student attendance appears to be more challenging. The districts in the study strove to improve attendance each summer without success. We believe that consistent summer attendance is inhibited by the following:

- a prevailing attitude that summer programs should be and are more relaxed than the school year, allowing for dropping in and out of the summer session
- a need for students to care for younger siblings at home
- changes to family plans and vacations
- student dislike of the program, which could be related to bullying or fighting among students, or to competing opportunities, which could be related to observing activities of friends and neighbors (who were not in the program).

We also found that high attenders had lower rates of eligibility for free or reduced-price meals, higher attendance rates the prior school year, and higher prior achievement. The racial and ethnic makeup of the two groups also differed, with the high-attendance group having more African-Americans and Asians and fewer Hispanics than the low-attendance group.

Perhaps there is more that could be done to address attendance barriers, including focusing on students who are likely to attend at lower rates. Districts may even want to consider mandatory programs for the lowest-performing students, who are less likely to attend the voluntary programs at high rates, although they arguably may need the program the most.

We also encourage practitioners to continue to improve the quality of summer programming, which may lead to higher attendance rates. In particular, program leaders should align their curriculum to both the school-year curriculum and state-level standards, while also ensuring that it meets the needs of the lowest-achieving students. The correlation we found between instructional quality and language arts outcomes implies that a focus on improving teaching effectiveness may also be worthwhile. In the sample of classes that we observed, despite small class sizes, not all teachers consistently checked for understanding or addressed misunderstandings when they arose. Encouraging teachers to take the time to ensure student understanding may accelerate students' summer learning.

Finally, the findings on no-show and inconsistent attendance rates can help districts better plan and reduce per-attender costs. By calculating the expected number of students using their own historical data or the expected no-show and average daily attendance rates identified in this study, districts can more accurately hire teachers, select facilities, and take other actions dependent on student numbers, thereby minimizing costs (ideally without adversely affecting components likely to have an impact on program effectiveness, such as small class sizes or program duration).

Next Steps

We will again examine academic, behavioral, and social-emotional outcomes in spring 2017, when these students reach the end of seventh grade, four years after randomization. We may discover that the impacts have dissipated, disappeared, persisted, or become stronger. This information will provide further evidence on the potential of these summer programs, as well as their cost-effectiveness.

We are also developing a report based on this study that will provide operational guidance for running summer programs. In addition, we are conducting a related set of studies that examine how summer influences students' learning trajectories, the policy context for summer programming, and the integration of summer programming and planning into districts' and communities' objectives and activities. These reports will be published over the next few years.

References

Allington, Richard L., Anne McGill-Franzen, Gregory Camilli, Lunetta Williams, Jennifer Graff, Jacqueline Zeig, Courtney Zmach, and Rhonda Nowak, "Addressing Summer Reading Setback Among Economically Disadvantaged Elementary Students," *Reading Psychology*, Vol. 31, No. 5, October 2010, pp. 411–427.

Arbreton, Amy J. A., Jean Baldwin Grossman, Carla Herrera, Leigh L. Linden, *Testing the Impact of Higher Achievement's Year-Round Out-of-School-Time Program on Academic Outcomes*, New York: Public/Private Ventures, 2011. As of March 21, 2016:
http://ppv.issuelab.org/resource/testing_the_impact_of_higher_achievements_year_round_out_of_school_time_program_on_academic_outcomes

Atteberry, Allison, Andrew McEachin, and Aryn Bloodworth, "School's Out: Summer Learning Loss Across Grade Levels and School Contexts in the U.S. Today," in K. Alexander, M. Boulay, and S. Pitcock, eds., *Summer Learning and Summer Learning Loss: Theory, Research and Practice*, New York: Teachers College Press, forthcoming.

Attendance Works, "What Works," web page, 2015. As of March 18, 2016:
http://www.attendanceworks.org/what-works/

Augustine, Catherine H., Jennifer Sloan McCombs, Heather L. Schwartz, and Laura Zakaras, *Getting to Work on Summer Learning: Recommended Practices for Success*, Santa Monica, Calif.: RAND Corporation, RR-366-WF, 2013. As of March 18, 2016:
http://www.rand.org/pubs/research_reports/RR366.html

Bailey, Drew, Greg J. Duncan, Candice Odgers, and Winnie Yu, *Persistence and Fadeout in the Impacts of Child and Adolescent Interventions*, Brisbane, Australia: ARC Centre of Excellence for Children and Families over the Life Course, Institute for Social Science Research, the University of Queensland, No. 2015-27, 2015. As of April 1, 2016:
https://espace.library.uq.edu.au/view/UQ:374173/UQ374173_OA.pdf

Baird, Matthew, John Engberg, Gerald Hunter, and Ben Master, *Trends in the Distribution of Teacher Effectiveness in the Intensive Partnerships for Effective Teaching Through 2014*, Santa Monica, Calif.: RAND Corporation, RR-1295/4-BMGF, 2016. As of July 13, 2016:
http://www.rand.org/pubs/research_reports/RR1295z4.html

Benson, James, and Geoffrey Borman, "Family, Neighborhood, and School Settings Across Seasons: When Do Socioeconomic Context and Racial Composition Matter for the Reading Achievement Growth of Young Children?" *Teachers College Record*, Vol. 112, No. 5, 2010, pp. 1338–1390.

Borman, Geoffrey D., James Benson, and Laura T. Overman, "Families, Schools, and Summer Learning," *Elementary School Journal*, Vol. 106, 2005, pp. 131–150.

Borman, Geoffrey D., and N. Maritza Dowling, "Longitudinal Achievement Effects of Multiyear Summer School: Evidence from the Teach Baltimore Randomized Field Trial," *Educational Evaluation and Policy Analysis*, Vol. 28, No. 1, 2006, pp. 25–48.

Borman, Geoffrey D., Michael Goetz, and N. Maritza Dowling, "Halting the Summer Achievement Slide: A Randomized Field Trial of the KindergARTen Summer Camp," *Journal of Education for Students Placed at Risk* (JESPAR), Vol. 14, No. 2, April 2009, pp. 133–147.

Bradshaw, Catherine P., Jessika H. Zmuda, Sheppard G. Kellam, and Nicholas S. Ialongo, "Longitudinal Impact of Two Universal Preventive Interventions in First Grade on Educational Outcomes in High School," *Journal of Educational Psychology*, Vol. 101, No. 4, 2009, pp. 926–937.

Campbell, Frances, Gabriella Conti, James J. Heckman, Seong Hyeok Moon, Rodrigo Pinto, Elizabeth Pungello, and Yi Pan, "Early Childhood Investments Substantially Boost Adult Health," *Science*, Vol. 343, No. 6178, 2014, pp. 1478–1485.

Chaplin, Duncan, and Jeffrey Capizzano, *Impacts of a Summer Learning Program: A Random Assignment Study of Building Educated Leaders for Life* (BELL), Washington, D.C.: Urban Institute, 2006.

Chetty, Raj, John N. Friedman, Nathaniel Hilger, Emmanuel Saez, Diane Whitmore Schanzenbach, and Danny Yagan, "How Does Your Kindergarten Classroom Affect Your Earnings? Evidence from Project STAR," *Quarterly Journal of Economics*, Vol. 126, No. 4, 2011, pp. 1593–1660.

Cheung, A. C. K., and R. E. Slavin, "How Methodological Features Affect Effect Sizes in Education," *Educational Researcher*, Vol. 45, No. 5, 2016, pp. 283–292.

Coleman, J. S., E. Q. Campbell, C. J. Hobson, J. McPartland, A. M. Mood, F. D. Weinfeld, et al., *Equality of Educational Opportunity*, Washington, D.C.: U.S. Government Printing Office, 1966.

Connor, Carol McDonald, and Frederick J. Morrison, "Individualizing Student Instruction in Reading: Implications for Policy and Practice," *Policy Insights from the Behavioral and Brain Sciences*, Vol. 3, No. 1, 2016, pp. 54–61.

Cooper, Harris, Kelly Charlton, Jeff C. Valentine, Laura Muhlenbruck, and Geoffrey D. Borman, *Making the Most of Summer School: A Meta-Analytic and Narrative Review*, Vol. 65, Monographs of the Society for Research in Child Development, Malden, Mass.: Blackwell Publishers, 2000.

Cooper, Harris, Barbara Nye, Kelly Charlton, James Lindsay, and Scott Greathouse, "The Effects of Summer Vacation on Achievement Test Scores: A Narrative and Meta-Analytic Review," *Review of Educational Research*, Vol. 66, No. 3, 1996, pp. 227–268.

Cornman, Stephen Q., *Documentation for the NCES Common Core of Data School District Finance Survey (F-33), School Year 2012–13 (Fiscal Year 2013)*, Provisional File Version 1a, Washington, D.C.: U.S. Department of Education, National Center for Education Statistics, 2015. As of April 1, 2016: https://nces.ed.gov/ccd/pdf/2015304.pdf

deJung, John E., and Kenneth Duckworth, "Measuring Student Absences in the High Schools," paper presented at the Annual Meeting of the American Educational Research Association, San Francisco, Calif., April 1986.

Downey, Douglas B., Paul T. Von Hippel, and Beckett A. Broh, "Are Schools the Great Equalizer? Cognitive Inequality During the Summer Months and the School Year," *American Sociological Review*, Vol. 69, No. 5, 2004, pp. 613–635.

ESSA — *See* Every Student Succeeds Act.

Every Student Succeeds Act, Section 8101, Definitions, December 10, 2015.

Fisher, Charles W., David C. Berliner, Nikola N. Filby, Richard Marliave, Leonard S. Cahen, and Marilyn M. Dishaw, "Teaching Behaviors, Academic Learning Time, and Student Achievement: An Overview," in Carolyn Denham and Ann Lieberman, eds., *Time to Learn: A Review of the Beginning Teacher Evaluation Study*, Sacramento, Calif.: California State Commission for Teacher Preparation and Licensing, 1980, pp. 7–32.

Gershenson, Seth, "Do Summer Time-Use Gaps Vary by Socioeconomic Status?" *American Educational Research Journal*, Vol. 50, No. 6, 2013, pp. 1219–1248.

Gottfredson, Gary D., and Denise C. Gottfredson, *School Climate, Academic Performance, Attendance, and Dropout*, ERIC Document Reproduction Service, No. ED 308225, 1989.

Guryan, Johnathan, James S. Kim, and Kyung Park, *Motivation and Incentives in Education: Evidence from a Summer Reading Experiment*, Cambridge, Mass.: National Bureau of Economic Research, NBER Working Paper 20918, 2015. As of March 21, 2016:
http://www.nber.org/papers/w20918

Harnischfeger, Annegret, and David E. Wiley, "The Teaching-Learning Process in Elementary Schools: A Synoptic View," *Curriculum Inquiry*, Vol. 6, No. 1, 1976, pp. 5–43.

Hawley, Willis D., Susan Rosenholtz, Henry J. Goodstein, and Ted Hasselbring, "Good Schools: What Research Says About Improving Student Achievement," *Peabody Journal of Education*, Vol. 61, No. 4, 1984, pp. iii–178.

Heyns, Barbara, *Summer Learning and the Effects of Schooling*, New York: Academic Press, 1979.

Jacob, Brian A., and Lars Lefgren, "Remedial Education and Student Achievement: A Regression-Discontinuity Design," *Review of Economics and Statistics*, Vol. 86, No. 1, 2004, pp. 226–244.

Karweit, Nancy, "Should We Lengthen the School Year?" *Educational Researcher*, Vol. 14, No. 6, 1985, pp. 9–15.

Karweit, Nancy, and Robert E. Slavin, "Time-on-Task: Issues of Timing, Sampling, and Definition," *Journal of Education Psychology*, Vol. 74, No. 6, 1982, pp. 844–851.

Kim, James S., "Summer Reading and the Ethnic Achievement Gap," *Journal of Education for Students Placed at Risk*, Vol. 9, No. 2, 2004, pp. 169–188.

———, "Effects of a Voluntary Summer Reading Intervention on Reading Achievement: Results From a Randomized Field Trial," *Educational Evaluation and Policy Analysis*, Vol. 28, No. 4, 2006, pp. 335–355.

Kim, James S., and Jonathan Guryan, "The Efficacy of a Voluntary Summer Book Reading Intervention for Low-Income Latino Children from Language Minority Families," *Journal of Educational Psychology*, Vol. 102, No. 1, 2010, pp. 20–31.

Kim, James S., and David M. Quinn, "The Effects of Summer Reading on Low-Income Children's Literacy Achievement from Kindergarten to Grade 8: A Meta-Analysis of Classroom and Home Interventions," *Review of Educational Research*, Vol. 83, No. 3, 2013, pp. 386–431.

Kim, James S., and Thomas G. White, "Scaffolding Voluntary Summer Reading for Children in Grades 3 to 5: An Experimental Study," *Scientific Studies of Reading*, Vol. 12, No. 1, 2008, pp. 1–23.

Lauer, Patricia A., Motoko Akiba, Stephanie B. Wilkerson, Helen S. Apthorp, David Snow, and Mya L. Martin-Glenn, "Out-of-School-Time Programs: A Meta-Analysis of Effects for At-Risk Students," *Review of Educational Research*, Vol. 76, No. 2, 2006, pp. 275–313.

Lipsey, Mark W., Kelly Puzio, Cathy Yun, Michael A. Hebert, Kasia Steinka-Fry, Mikel W. Cole, Megan Roberts, Karen S. Anthony, and Matthew D. Busick, *Translating the Statistical Representation of the Effects of Education Interventions into More Readily Interpretable Forms*, Washington, D.C.: National Center for Special Education Research, Institute of Education Sciences, U.S. Department of Education, NCSER 2013-3000, 2012.

Lomax, Richard G., and William W. Cooley, "The Student Achievement-Instructional Time Relationship," paper presented at the Annual Meeting of the American Educational Research Association, San Francisco, Calif., April 1979.

Martorell, Paco, Trey Miller, Lucrecia Santibañez, and Catherine H. Augustine, "Can Incentives for Parents and Students Change Educational Inputs? Experimental Evidence from Summer School," *Economics of Education Review*, Vol. 50, 2016, pp. 113–126.

Matsudaira, Jordan D., "Mandatory Summer School and Student Achievement," *Journal of Econometrics*, Vol. 142, No. 2, 2008, pp. 829–850.

McCoach, D. Betsy, Ann A. O'Connell, Sally M. Reis, and Heather A. Levitt, "Growing Readers: A Hierarchical Linear Model of Children's Reading Growth During the First 2 Years of School," *Journal of Educational Psychology*, Vol. 98, No. 1, 2006, pp. 14–28.

McCombs, Jennifer Sloan, Sheila Nataraj Kirby, and Louis T. Mariano, eds., *Ending Social Promotion Without Leaving Children Behind: The Case of New York City*, Santa Monica, Calif.: RAND Corporation, MG-894-NYCDOE, 2009. As of March 21, 2016:
http://www.rand.org/pubs/monographs/MG894.html

McCombs, Jennifer Sloan, John F. Pane, Catherine H. Augustine, Heather L. Schwartz, Paco Martorell, and Laura Zakaras, *Ready for Fall? Near-Term Effects of Voluntary Summer Learning Programs on Low-Income Students' Learning Opportunities and Outcomes*, Santa Monica, Calif.: RAND Corporation, RR-815-WF, 2014. As of March 18, 2016:
http://www.rand.org/pubs/research_reports/RR815.html

Nansel, Tonja R., Mary Overpeck, Ramani S. Pilla, W. June Ruan, Bruce Simons-Morton, and Peter Scheidt, "Bullying Behaviors Among U.S. Youth: Prevalence and Association With Psychosocial Adjustment," *Journal of American Medical Association*, Vol. 285, No. 16, 2001, pp. 2094–2100.

National Center for Education Statistics, "Table 2. Public High School 4-Year Adjusted Cohort Graduation Rate (ACGR), by Race/Ethnicity and Selected Demographics for the United States, the 50 states, and the District of Columbia: School Year 2012–13," *EDFacts/Consolidated State Performance Report, SY 2012–13*, Washington, D.C.: U.S. Department of Education, February 2015. As of July 25, 2015:
https://nces.ed.gov/ccd/tables/ACGR_RE_and_characteristics_2012-13.asp

Pell Institute, *Indicators of Higher Education Equity in the United States—45 Year Trend Report*, Washington, D.C., 2015. As of July 21, 2015:
http://www.pellinstitute.org/publications-Indicators_of_Higher_Education_Equity_in_the_United_States_45_Year_Report.shtml

Pew Research Center, *Parenting in America: Outlook, Worries, Aspirations Are Strongly Linked to Financial Situation*, Washington, D.C., December 17, 2015. As of April 12, 2016:
http://www.pewsocialtrends.org/files/2015/12/2015-12-17_parenting-in-america_FINAL.pdf

Protzko, John, "The Environment in Raising Early Intelligence: A Meta-Analysis of the Fadeout Effect," *Intelligence*, Vol. 53, 2015, pp. 202–210.

Puma, Michael, Stephen Bell, Ronna Cook, Camilla Heid, Pam Broene, Frank Jenkins, and Jason Downer, *Third Grade Follow-Up to the Head Start Impact Study: Final Report*, Washington, D.C.: Office of Planning, Research, and Evaluation, Administration for Children and Families, U.S. Department of Health and Human Services, OPRE Report 2012-45, 2012.

Purkey, Stewart C., and Marshall S. Smith, "Effective Schools: A Review," *Elementary School Journal*, Vol. 83, No. 4, 1983, pp. 427–454.

Ready, Douglas D., "Socioeconomic Disadvantage, School Attendance, and Early Cognitive Development: The Differential Effects of School Exposure," *Sociology of Education*, Vol. 83, No. 4, 2010, pp. 271–286.

Reardon, Sean F., Joseph P. Robinson-Cimpian, and Ericka S. Weathers, "Patterns and Trends in Racial/Ethnic and Socioeconomic Achievement Gaps," in Helen F. Ladd and Margaret E. Goertz, eds., *Handbook of Research in Education Finance and Policy*, 2nd edition, New York: Routledge, 2015, pp. 491–509.

Reid, Ken, "Retrospection and Persistent School Absenteeism," *Educational Research*, Vol. 25, No. 2, 1983, pp. 110–115.

Rumberger, Russell W., "High School Dropouts: A Review of Issues and Evidence," *Review of Educational Research*, Vol. 57, No. 2, Summer 1987, pp. 101–121.

Schacter, John, and Booil Jo, "Learning When School Is Not in Session: A Reading Summer Day-Camp Intervention to Improve the Achievement of Exiting First-Grade Students Who Are Economically Disadvantaged," *Journal of Research in Reading*, Vol. 28, No. 2, 2005, pp. 158–169.

Schweinhart, Lawrence J., Jeanne Montie, Zongping Xiang, W. Steven Barnett, Clive R. Belfield, and Milagros Nores, *Lifetime Effects: The High/Scope Perry Preschool Study Through Age 40*, Ypsilanti, Mich.: High/Scope Press, 2005.

Smith, BetsAnn, *It's About Time: Opportunities to Learn in Chicago's Elementary Schools*, Chicago, Ill.: Consortium on Chicago School Research, 1998. As of March 11, 2016: https://consortium.uchicago.edu/sites/default/files/publications/p0f03.pdf

Snipes, Jason, Chung-Wei Huang, Karina Jaquet, and Neal Finkelstein, *The Effects of the Elevate Math Summer Program on Math Achievement and Algebra Readiness*, Washington, D.C.: U.S. Department of Education, Institute of Education Sciences, REL 2015–096, 2015. As of March 21, 2016: http://ies.ed.gov/ncee/edlabs/regions/west/pdf/REL_2015096.pdf

Somers, Marie-Andrée, Rashida Welbeck, Jean B. Grossman, and Susan Gooden, *An Analysis of the Effects of an Academic Summer Program for Middle School Students*, New York: MDRC, 2015.

Sommer, Barbara, "What's Different About Truants? A Comparison Study of Eighth Graders," *Journal of Youth and Adolescence*, Vol. 14, No. 5, 1985, pp. 411–422.

U.S. Bureau of Labor Statistics, "Earnings and Unemployment Rates by Educational Attainment," *Current Population Survey*, Washington, D.C.: U.S. Department of Labor, 2014.

U.S. Department of Education, *What Works Clearinghouse: Procedures and Standards Handbook* (Version 3.0), Washington, D.C.: Institute of Education Sciences, 2014.

———, *The Nations Report Card, 2015 Mathematics & Reading Assessments*, 2015. As of April 12, 2016: http://www.nationsreportcard.gov/reading_math_2015/#?grade=4

Von Hippel, Peter T., Caitlin Hamrock, and Mina Kumar, *Do Test Score Gaps Grow Before, During or Between the School Years? Measurement Artifacts and What We Can Know in Spite of Them*, working paper, Social Science Research Network, 2016.

White, Thomas G., James S. Kim, Helen Chen Kingston, and Lisa Foster, "Replicating the Effects of a Teacher-Scaffolded Voluntary Summer Reading Program: The Role over Poverty," *Reading Research Quarterly*, Vol. 49, No. 1, 2014, pp. 5–30.

Wilkins, Chuck, Russell Gersten, Lauren E. Decker, Leslie Grunden, Sarah Brasiel, Kim Brunnert, and Madhavi Jayanthi, *Does a Summer Reading Program Based on Lexiles Affect Reading Comprehension?* Washington, D.C.: U.S. Department of Education, NCEE 2012-4006, March 2012. As of July 18, 2016:
http://ies.ed.gov/ncee/edlabs/regions/southwest/pdf/REL_20124006.pdf

Yeh, Stuart S., "The Cost Effectiveness of 22 Approaches for Raising Student Achievement," *Journal of Education Finance*, Vol. 36, No. 1, 2010, pp. 38–75.